BISHOPS

A CONCISE STUDY

MARTIN DAVIE

The Latimer Trust

ISBN 978-1-906327-77-4 Published by the Latimer Trust September 2022.

The Latimer Trust (formerly Latimer House, Oxford) is a conservative Evangelical research organisation within the Church of England, whose main aim is to promote the history and theology of Anglicanism as understood by those in the Reformed tradition. Interested readers are welcome to consult its website for further details of its many activities.

The Latimer Trust
London N14 4PS UK
Registered Charity: 1084337
Company Number: 4104465
Web: www.latimertrust.org
E-mail: administrator@latimertrust.org

This brilliant little book is the essential conclusions of Martin Davie's larger book *'Bishops, Past Present and Future'*. With wide ranging scholarship, it helpfully addresses the important question 'what kind of bishops do we need?' It re-establishes the Reformation case for Anglican polity, and will cause people to think again about their ecclesiology. Most importantly, it is a call for current bishops to behave like the early bishops who were powerful advocates of Apostolic faith and practice. The Church would greatly benefit if every bishop and church leader read this!

Wallace Benn, former Bishop of Lewes

Episcopacy is one of the defining characteristics of the Anglican Communion but despite its importance, there are few studies that explain all the ramifications of the office of a bishop as Anglicans have received it and as they put it into practice. In this study, Martin Davie provides us with a comprehensive but accessible guide to the subject, making it clear why it matters and offering suggestions for dealing with the issues it raises for us at the present time.

Gerald Bray, Research Professor Beeson Divinity School, Samford University, Birmingham, AL

CONTENTS PAGE

Foreword for the Leadership Series   I

Preface   3

Introduction   5

1. Why the Church of England should have   7
bishops and what the role and character of
bishops should be

2. 'Good-enough' and 'not good enough'   25
bishops

3. The challenges facing bishops today because   37
of the secularisation of Western society

4. Back to the future: how bishops should meet   71
the challenges of our day

Foreword for the Leadership Series

This booklet is the first in a new series from Latimer Trust, where we will be exploring various aspects of Christian leadership. Whilst we have done work in this area before (and you can find these books listed on our website under 'Books on Christian Leadership') we believe that more attention needs to be given to this important subject. In beginning this series, we are guided by three considerations.

First, and critically, we offer these words as reflective contributions to the current debate on what Christian leadership should looks like, particularly in churches. We are seeking to open the subjects up for thorough discussion, not 'solve' leadership in a short booklet.

Second, we recognize that this is a broad and complex area and requires serious and deep reflection. Therefore, we will be exploring it from a variety of perspectives: biblically, theologically, historically, and in the context of current cultural contexts and issues. Individual studies will have a narrower focus, but the aims of the series as a whole are broad.

Third, as an Anglican organization committed to bringing 'Biblical Truth for Today's Church', we will give attention to the application of these leadership issues within the Anglican tradition and polity

Our hope is that we can encourage all those involved in Christian leadership, whether of churches or within churches, to seek to more biblically grounded, theologically aware, and historically literate as we face the challenges of leadership in the 21st century.

James Hughes

PREFACE

Evangelical Christians will always want to focus their ministry on the local congregation. However if they are concerned about the longer term welfare of their church family then they cannot be oblivious to their wider connections. Amongst Anglicans this inevitably involves dealing with bishops and thinking carefully about their role as the senior leaders of the church. The actions of bishops matter, yet ignorant and ill-informed comment on them is not helpful and will not promote the gospel of the Lord Jesus Christ.

The problem is that the history of the role of bishops and how they relate to the government of God's people in New Testament times is very complex. That is why this concise study by Martin Davie is so very welcome. It serves as a way into his larger volume which deals in detail with the questions many have about the proper role of bishops. Nevertheless this concise study can stand in its own right as enabling thoughtful Christians to find answers to the key questions that are likely to arise today.

In this booklet Martin clarifies what bishops are called to do and the kind of people they should be. In the present day confusion these priorities are often lost sight of. In connection with this he also explains the more specific nature of jurisdiction and how that fits with the universal role that bishops are called to.

We are then introduced to the concept of 'good enough' and 'not good enough' bishops. And in the case of the latter Martin carefully distinguishes between different categories of 'not good enough' bishops. Following a sketch of the particular challenges involved in following Christ faithfully in our modern secular society we find the earlier material is applied through an agenda for bishops today and in the future. Here we see an outline of how orthodox bishops can exercise a faithful ministry in the present Anglican context. The focus of this is found in a variety of possible scenarios emerging from the pressure for the endorsement of same sex relationships in some form or another. Naturally this also provides guidance as to how all orthodox Christians should respond if ungodly behaviour and teaching is promoted.

This booklet is a vital resource for all Anglicans who want to understand the history and wisdom of church government through episcopacy and then apply that understanding to church life today. It will thus strengthen the life and witness of many Anglican congregations.

Mark Burkill

Introduction

It is a little-known fact, but the farewell advice of the Reformer John Knox to the Church of Scotland was that what the Kirk needed was more and better bishops. The lesson I take from Knox's farewell words is that bishops matter. It matters that churches should have bishops and it matters that those bishops perform their episcopal calling in a proper manner and to the best of their ability.

I have been studying episcopacy in general, and episcopacy in the Church of England in particular, for over twenty years, first as the Theological Secretary to the Church of England's Council for Christian Unity and Theological Consultant to its House of Bishops and latterly as a Latimer Trust Fellow and Theological Consultant to the Church of England Evangelical Council.

In the course of my work on this subject it has become ever clearer to me that the majority of people in the Church of England, including many people who are otherwise theologically well-informed, are confused about the answers to three key questions: 'Why should the Church of England have bishops?' 'What is the proper role of bishops?' and 'How should bishops respond to the challenges facing the Church of England and the Church in the West in general today?'

In order to provide answers to these questions, I have written a major study of episcopacy which has been published earlier this year by Gilead Books under the title *Bishops Past, Present and Future.*[1]

A number of those who read the draft text of this study suggested that because of its length and complexity it would be good to publish its final chapter as a stand-alone text. This small book is my response to this suggestion. It is an adapted version of the final chapter that is designed to present the key points of my argument to those who would balk at tackling the 800+ pages of my original study.

My hope is that it will help many in the Church of England to think in a more informed fashion about how bishops should respond to the challenges facing the Church of England at this critical point in its history as it considers how to move forward following the publication of the *Living in Love and Faith* material.

---

[1] Martin Davie, *Bishops Past Present and Future* (Malton: Gilead Books, 2022).

1. WHY THE CHURCH OF ENGLAND SHOULD HAVE BISHOPS AND WHAT THE ROLE AND CHARACTER OF BISHOPS SHOULD BE

We can summarise the reason why the Church has had bishops by saying that the first bishops of the Church were the apostles themselves, and the apostles then appointed other bishops to succeed them in the role of exercising pastoral oversight over the clergy and laity of the churches they had founded.

This is the view that has traditionally been taken in the Church of England and that finds expression in the famous words of the preface to the 1662 *Ordinal*:

> It is evident to all men diligently reading holy Scripture and ancient Authors, that from the Apostles' time there have been these Orders of ministers in Christ's Church; Bishops, Priests and Deacons.

Until the sixteenth century there does not seem to have been anybody who would have questioned the truth of this statement. People disagreed about the precise reasons why the apostles introduced bishops, and the precise nature of the distinction between priests/presbyters and bishops, but no one seems to have doubted that the practice of having bishops was of apostolic origin. However, from the sixteenth century onwards this traditional consensus has been completely reversed with the scholarly consensus

7

today, including among Anglican scholars, being that the apostles did not institute episcopacy, but that bishops were first introduced into the Church in the second century in response to the challenges the Church was facing at that time. However, study of the relevant evidence shows that the traditional consensus was correct, and the modern consensus is wrong.

The origins of the episcopate

In the New Testament itself and in the two earliest post New Testament writings known as the *Didache* and *1 Clement* the two terms *presbuteros* (elder/presbyter) and *episkopos* (bishop) are used as synonyms (see Acts 20:17 & 28, Philippians 1:1, 1 Timothy 3:1-7 & 5:7-19, Titus 1:3-7 and 1 Peter 5:2). However, although the term *episkopos* is thus not used in the New Testament to refer to the distinctive form of ministry which would later be called episcopacy, the evidence we have indicates that such a ministry existed in New Testament times.

Episcopal oversight, in the sense of the overall oversight or 'government' of the churches, was first exercised by the apostles themselves. In the words of the sixteenth century Anglican writer Richard Hooker:

> They which were termed Apostles, as being sent of Christ to publish his gospel throughout the world, and were named likewise Bishops, in that the care of government was also committed unto them, did no less perform the offices of their episcopal authority by

governing, than of their apostolical by teaching.[2]

The apostles' episcopal oversight was originally universal in extent (see Matthew 28:18-20), but the geographical areas in which they exercised oversight gradually became divided up, and the combined evidence of the New Testament, the other sources which we have from the first and second centuries, and later writings such as Eusebius' *Ecclesiastical History,* tells us that the apostles gradually appointed others to exercise episcopal oversight over churches for which they had originally been personally responsible. In this way James was given episcopal oversight over the Church in Jerusalem, Timothy was given episcopal oversight in Ephesus, Titus was given episcopal oversight in Crete, and the angels of the churches in Revelation 2 and 3 were given episcopal oversight over the seven churches of Asia.[3] This means that although

---

[2] Richard Hooker, *The Laws of Ecclesiastical Polity* Bk. VII.iv.1 (Oxford: OUP, 1841), pp. 336-337.

[3] The Episcopal role of the angels in Revelation 2-3 is helpfully unpacked by the Elizabethan writer Thomas Bilson, who writes that we need to ask:

.... how the Son of God could write precisely to one angel in every of those seven churches, if there were many or none? And what reason to charge him above the rest; if he had no pastoral power besides the rest? It is therefore evident the churches of Christ before that time were guided by certain chief pastors, that moderated as well the presbyters as the rest of the flock; and those the Son of God

the term 'bishop' (*episkopos*) is first used as a specific title for those exercising this sort of episcopal oversight in the letters of Ignatius at the beginning of the second century, the office to which the title refers seems to have existed, at least as far as the church in Jerusalem is concerned, from very early on in the Church's history. Thus, James appears to have already been Bishop of Jerusalem by the time of Peter's miraculous escape from prison recorded in Acts 12.

From the second century onwards, we find no evidence for the existence of any church that did not have an episcopal form of church government and the universal consensus, reflected by early writers such as Irenaeus, Hegesippus and Tertullian, was that later bishops were in a line of historical succession that could be traced back to the apostles themselves. For instance, Timothy was understood to have been appointed as the first bishop of Ephesus by Paul and all subsequent bishops of Ephesus traced their episcopal lineage back through to Timothy to Paul. The accuracy of these lines of historic episcopal succession has been questioned by church historians, but no good reason has been produced to show that they are incorrect and the evidence for them can be traced back to the

---

acknowledgeth for stars and angels, that is for messengers and stewards of the Lord of Hosts; at whose mouth the rest should ask and receive the knowledge of God's divine will and pleasure. (Thomas Bilson, *The Perpetual Government of Christ's Church* (Oxford: OUP, 1842), p. 367).

testimony of people who were still alive in the time of the apostles.

A sharp distinction is often drawn between the Church of the first century and the church of the second century. However, this sharp distinction is historically unrealistic for several reasons.

First, John and possibly others of the apostles seem to have lived on in Asia Minor until the start of the second century. Secondly, early second century figures such as Ignatius of Antioch and Polycarp of Smyrna seem to have been born and grown to adulthood during the latter years of the first century. Thirdly, even in the second half of the second century there were those such as Hegesippus and Irenaeus who were born towards the beginning of the second century and who would know those who had lived during the apostolic era. Fourthly, even those born in the second half of the second century, such as Clement of Alexandria and Tertullian, would have known people who had known people with first-hand knowledge of the practice of the apostolic Church. They were only two generations away from the apostolic age.

All this being so, the best explanation for the universal second century belief that the apostles had appointed the first bishops and that subsequent bishops were their successors is that this was actually the case.

Furthermore, this explanation coheres with the evidence from the New Testament and other early sources which points to the existence of bishops appointed by the apostles in the churches of the first century from the time of the appointment of James as the first Bishop of Jerusalem. The evidence we have for the second century follows on seamlessly from this evidence we have for the first century.

Dioceses, provinces and patriarchs

From the earliest times, bishops had responsibility for more than one church, with James, Timothy, Titus, and the angels of the churches having responsibility for multiple churches in Jerusalem, Ephesus, Crete and the seven cities referred to in Revelation (such groups of churches constituting what later came to be called dioceses). During the second century ecclesiastical provinces made up of the dioceses overseen by a group of bishops were formed based on the civil provinces of the Roman Empire. During the third century the bishop of the metropolitan city of the province (the 'metropolitan' bishop) came to be viewed as having a position of superiority over the other bishops of the province and he was referred to as the 'arch' or chief bishop to mark his consequent superiority. Finally, a further distinction emerged between the metropolitans, with the bishops of the most important metropolitan cities being given the titles of primates and patriarchs. In the councils of the fourth century the bishops of Rome, Alexandria, Antioch and Constantinople were acknowledged as having this patriarchal position.

Episcopacy in the Church of England

Such documentary and archaeological evidence as we have indicates that the Church in Roman Britain was episcopal from the outset and that by the fourth century it had its own system of provinces and metropolitan bishoprics.[4] This provincial system collapsed following the Saxon conquest of most of England from the fifth century onwards. However, following the emergence of a new English church (the 'Church of England') as a result of the evangelization of the Saxon kingdoms led by missionary bishops from Europe and from the Scottish Celtic tradition, a new diocesan and provincial system eventually emerged in the eighth century with two provinces, one southern and one northern, presided over by the two archbishops of Canterbury and York.

The episcopal and provincial system instituted during the early Saxon period was deliberately and carefully maintained in the centuries that followed, even in the face of the religious and political turmoil of the Reformation, the English Civil War and the Commonwealth. As a result, all the dioceses of the present-day Church of England (except for the diocese

---

[4] The records of the Synod of Arles in 314 tell us that the British church was represented by three bishops: 'Eborius, Bishop of the City of York in the province of Britain. Restitutus, Bishop of the City of London in the province above written. Adelfius, Bishop of the City Colonia Londinensium' (Text in H Gee and W R Hardy (eds.) *Documents illustrative of the History of the English Church* (London: Macmillan 1896) p. 1). It has been plausibly suggested that these were metropolitan bishops representing the bishops of three out of the four Roman provinces into which Roman Britain was then divided.

of Sodor and Man which originally formed part of a Norwegian diocese) can trace their origins back to the original dioceses of the Saxon Church of England and all the bishops of the Church of England can trace their episcopal lineage back to the first bishops of that church and through them to the first bishops appointed by the apostles themselves.

Why it is right for the Church to have bishops

The tendency of the Church of England in recent times has been to argue that it is right to have bishops because episcopacy is the historic form of church government and bishops perform a variety of useful practical and symbolic functions in the life of the Church. However, we also saw that these are not the fundamental reason why it is right for the Church of England (and all other churches) to have bishops in historic succession.

The fundamental reason is that an episcopal system of church government was introduced by the apostles, who were acting with the authority of God. To quote once again the words of Hooker:

> ... whether the Apostles alone did conclude of such a regiment, or else they together with the whole Church judging it a fit and a needful policy did agree to receive it for a custom; no doubt but being established by them on whom the Holy Ghost was poured in so abundant measure for the ordering of Christ's Church, it had either divine appointment beforehand, or divine approbation afterwards, and is in that respect to be acknowledged the ordinance of

God, no less than the ancient Jewish regiment, whereof though Jethro were the deviser (Exodus 18: 19), yet after that God had allowed it, all men were subject unto it, as to the polity of God, and not of Jethro.[5]

A church which wants to be faithful to the pattern of church government ordained by God himself through the apostles should therefore have bishops, and it would make sense for these bishops to be consecrated in historic succession (as happened at the English Reformation) as a visible sign that these bishops are intended to be in continuity with the bishops who were first appointed by the apostles.

This does not mean, however, that having bishops is a benchmark by which it can be decided whether a particular group of people is a church at all. As Article XIX of the *Thirty Nine Articles* explains, there are two 'essential' notes of the church, the true preaching of the word and the right administration of the sacraments, and from this it follows that a church that has these two notes is a church, regardless of the kind of government it has. It would be better if it had bishops, but it is nonetheless still a church, and the Church of England would be able to recognise it as such.

For the detailed evidence for what has been said thus far see *Bishops Past, Present and Future* chapters 1-6.

---

[5] Hooker, Bk. VII.5.2., p. 341.

What bishops are called to do and what sort of people they need to be

Church of England writings from the twentieth and twenty-first centuries contain a variety of different accounts of the role and character of bishops. However, despite this variety, if we consider these accounts as a whole, we find that a coherent picture of the bishop's role and character emerges from them. This picture can be summarised as follows.

In terms of what bishops are called to do:

    a.   Bishops are called to be Pastors to all in their dioceses, whether clergy or lay, whether in the Church or outside it.

    b.   They are to be guardians of the Christian faith as the Church of England has received it and to oppose error.

    c.   They are to be leaders of the Church's mission in the world.

    d.   They are to teach and preach.

    e.   They are to lead worship, preside at the celebration of the sacraments and confirm.

    f.   They are to promote unity in their dioceses and in the wider Church and encourage peace and reconciliation in the Church and the world.

    g.   They are to care for the poor and needy.

    h.   They are to ensure that there are sufficient ordained and authorised lay ministers in their dioceses and ordain and licence them to undertake their ministries.

    i.   They are to take part in the ordination and consecration of other bishops

j. They are to exercise ecclesiastical discipline and absolve the penitent.
k. They are to ensure that church buildings and churchyards are properly maintained and renovated.
l. They are to take counsel together with other bishops and with clergy and lay people in the synods, boards, and councils of their diocese and of the national church, using their power of veto when necessary.

In terms of the kind of people bishops are to be:

a. Bishops are to be baptized disciples of Jesus Christ.
b. They are to be deacons and priests before they are bishops and to continue a diaconal and priestly ministry as bishops.
c. They are to be people who personally accept the Christian faith as the Church of England has received it and committed to upholding and proclaiming it.
d. They are to be people with the ability to preach, teach and lead worship.
e. They are to be people of prayer who spend time studying the Scriptures and other writings that will enable them to understand and proclaim the faith.
f. They are to be people who have the capacity to understand new developments in the Church and in the world and interpret them in the light of the Bible and the orthodox Christian tradition.

A comparison of this picture with the teaching about the role and character of bishops which can be found in the New Testament, in the writings of the Patristic period and in Church of England writings from the sixteenth and seventeenth centuries, including the normative 1662 *Ordinal,* shows that there is a continuity between this picture and this earlier teaching. The Church of England has remained a traditional church in its understanding of the role and character of bishops, just as much as it has remained a traditional church by continuing to have bishops in historic succession.

The role of the Bishop of Rome

A study of the New Testament and the Patristic tradition about the specific role of the Bishop of Rome shows that there is a straight line of historical continuity between the claims for the universal Petrine authority of the Pope made by Pope Leo I in the mid fifth century and the claims for the authority of the Pope contained in the two key modern Roman Catholic documents on the topic, *Pastor Aeternus* in 1870 and *Lumen Gentium* in 1964. However, what we also discovered is that there is no direct line of historical continuity that extends back from the teaching of Pope Leo through the writings of the Fathers of the first five centuries to the ministry given to Peter by Christ. Although from New Testament times onwards the Church of Rome was regarded as a very important church, it is only at the end of the fourth century that the idea came to be put forward by the Popes that the bishops of Rome had an unquestionable authority over the Church as a whole based on the commission given by Christ to Peter. This was a new idea, and it was not one that was ever accepted by the ecumenical councils, or by the Church as whole.

The claims for the Papacy made by the Roman Catholic Church thus fail the test of Catholicity in that they are not part of the apostolic witness contained in the New Testament, or the teaching of the Early Fathers, and they have never been accepted across the Church as whole. The Church of England was therefore right to reject these claims at the time of the Reformation.

Episcopal Jurisdiction

Being a bishop involves exercising what is known as 'episcopal jurisdiction.'

The term 'jurisdiction' means both the official legal authority a person, or group of persons, possesses either to do something themselves, or to command something to be done (or not done) by others, and the area over which this authority extends. The purpose of episcopal jurisdiction is the building up of the body of the Church as the body of Christ in the way described by Paul in Ephesians 4:11-16.

By virtue of their episcopal orders bishops have in principle the same kind of universal jurisdiction originally given to the apostles, but that the exercise of this universal jurisdiction is normally limited by the Church to specific places to avoid confusion and conflicting claims to authority. However, it has also been accepted by the Church as a whole, and by the

Church of England and the Anglican Communion, that bishops may act outside the normal limits of their jurisdiction if circumstances mean that it would be right for them to do so. In the words of the Catholic writer Zeger Van-Espen:

> The jurisdiction of the bishops is circumscribed within certain limits for the greater commodity of the Church: but when this end ceases, and it is rather for the advantage of the Church that a bishop should go beyond the boundaries of his jurisdiction, he can freely do so.[6]

In addition, parallel episcopal jurisdictions should not exist because they violate the principle established by the apostles and upheld by the Early Church that there should be one bishop and one church in each geographical area. In normal circumstances Christians should work to bring parallel episcopal jurisdictions to an end. However, it may also be necessary to establish new ones in emergency situations where a bishop is unable, or unwilling, to proclaim the gospel to those outside the Church, or to provide appropriate pastoral care for those inside it, or where a bishop or church has fallen into heresy and faithful Christians need to separate themselves from that bishop or that church as a result.

---

[6] Zeger Van-Espen, *Dissertatio de Misero Statu Ecclesiae Ultrajectinae*, quoted in F W Puller, *Orders and Jurisdiction* (London: Longman, Green and Co, 1925), p. 154.

We further noted that in the Early Church metropolitan and patriarchal jurisdictions came into existence alongside diocesan jurisdictions. However, these jurisdictions were limited both in extent and the degree of authority involved, and action taken outside of these limits was viewed as unacceptable. It was for this reason that the claims for universal and unlimited jurisdiction made by the Popes from the end of the fourth century were regarded as illegitimate by the churches in the Eastern Empire and Africa.

In the Church of England bishops exercise their jurisdiction in personal, collegial and communal ways, acting as individuals, but also in collaboration with other bishops, other members of the clergy and with the laity. Following the rejection of Papal jurisdiction at the Reformation, there is no higher jurisdiction in the Church of England than the legal jurisdiction exercised by the Queen as the Church of England's supreme governor and the metropolitical jurisdictions exercised by the Archbishops of Canterbury and York.

In the Anglican Communion each province has its own diocesan and metropolitan bishops, but there is no bishop with jurisdiction over the Communion as whole. The Archbishop of Canterbury has certain specific roles within the Communion, but he is not the Anglican equivalent of the Pope and has no power to determine the teaching or practice of the Anglican Communion. These are determined on a collegial and communal basis, by the Lambeth Conference, the Primates Meeting and the Anglican Consultative Council. Contemporary Anglican ecumenical thinking has become open to the possibility of the Pope acting as a world-wide personal focus of unity in a re-united Church. However, Anglicans are still unhappy, or at best cautious, about the claim made by the Popes for a world- wide Petrine jurisdiction.

When exercising their jurisdiction bishops are subject to a range of laws. They are subject to Scripture, which is God's word written, and which uniquely reveals the way of eternal salvation through Jesus Christ. However, they are also subject to the law of nature, the law of reason, the law of the Church and the law of the state. While bishops should normally obey the laws of the Church and the state, they should be prepared to disobey them if they go against the law of God as revealed in Scripture. Similarly, bishops should support appropriate changes in the laws of the Church and the state to meet new circumstances, but only if these changes do not contravene the law of God.

Suffragan bishops

The distinction between episcopal orders and jurisdiction enables us to make sense of the distinction between diocesan bishops and suffragan bishops, that is bishops who give assistance to their diocesan bishop.

The evidence from Patristic sources tells us that there were suffragan bishops from the second century onwards and that there were two types of such bishops. There were coadjutor bishops who assisted aged or infirm diocesan bishops with the expectation that they would succeed them, and there were rural bishops (*chorepiscopi*) who served in the rural areas of dioceses under the jurisdiction of the diocesan.

In the Church of England there were suffragan bishops in the Middle Ages whose responsibility it was to undertake the spiritual responsibilities of diocesan bishops, especially ordaining and confirming, when the latter were absent from their dioceses. At the Reformation provision was made for the appointment of suffragan bishops by the *Suffragan Bishops Act* of 1534, and although the practice of appointing suffragan bishops lapsed at the beginning of the seventeenth century it was revived in 1870, and today there are more suffragan bishops in the Church of England than diocesan bishops.

Today suffragan bishops in the Church of England are bishops who exercise particular roles within dioceses under the authority of the diocesan bishop. These roles may be exercised across a diocese, or mainly exercised in a particular area of a diocese in what are known as 'area schemes.' The five Provincial Episcopal Visitors are suffragan bishops whose role is to provide episcopal ministry to parishes that wish to receive priestly or episcopal ministry from men rather than women.

There has been debate about the ministry of suffragan bishops and how it relates to that of diocesan bishops since Patristic times. This debate continues in the Church of England today and is reflected in the different models for the ministry of suffragan bishops put forward by the two Church of England reports *Episcopal Ministry* and *Suffragan*

Bishops. The former sees a suffragan bishop as an 'episcopal vicar' exercising ministry on behalf of his or her diocesan. The latter sees a suffragan bishop as a member of a college of bishops, the members of which exercise episcopal ministry in a diocese on an equal basis. We noted that there are serious problems with both these models, and that a better approach is to see the distinction between diocesan and suffragan bishops in terms of jurisdiction.

A suffragan bishop is like all other bishops in virtue of his or her orders and hence is able to exercise the full range of episcopal ministry. However, a suffragan bishop is distinguished from a diocesan bishop in that he or she is given jurisdiction to exercise his or her ministry in a particular diocese, under the authority of its diocesan, and in a manner laid down by that diocesan.

This understanding of the suffragan bishop's role preserves the truth that a suffragan bishop exercises his or her own ministry, while at the same time preserving monepiscopacy, the principle that there is one bishop with overall responsibility for the oversight of each diocese.

For the detailed evidence for what is said in the second half of this chapter see *Bishops Past, Present and Future*, Chapters 7-13.

2. 'Good-enough' and 'not good enough' bishops

'Good-enough' bishops[7]

The continuing presence of sin in the life of every Christian means that no bishop ever exercises their ministry in a perfect fashion. Every bishop always falls short.[8] Nevertheless, there can be bishops who

---

7 ' I have taken the term 'good-enough bishop' from Paul Avis's book *Becoming a Bishop* ((London: Bloomsbury/T&T Clark, 2015) in which he writes of the importance of the 'good-enough' bishop in the life of the Church:

> A good-enough bishop is a precious gift of God to God's Church. While it is true that some dioceses revive after the bishop has moved on - just as some parishes spring back to life after the departure of their priest, whose presence acted like a wet blanket on lay initiative - a good bishop is a source of strength, inspiration and wisdom to his or her people. Bishops can make a qualitative difference for good or ill, to how church people experience their faith, worship and witness from day to day.(p. 13)

8 The imperfection of their episcopal ministry is something that has been generally accepted by godly bishops since the earliest days of the Church. For example, it is what underlies Augustine's famous comment in Sermon 340 'for you I am a bishop, with you, after all, I am a Christian'. The full quotation, of which these words are part, runs as follows:

But you too must all support me, so that according to the apostle's instructions we may carry one another's burdens,

are 'good-enough' because, despite their imperfections, they exercise their episcopal jurisdiction in a generally adequate fashion.

Such bishops need, first, to be pastors. This means that they need to feed the sheep of Christ's flock with the spiritual food of the Christian faith, protect them

---

and in this way fulfil the law of Christ (Galatians 6:2). If he doesn't carry it with us, we collapse; if he doesn't carry us, we keel over and die. Where I'm terrified by what I am for you, I am given comfort by what I am with you. For you I am a bishop, with you, after all, I am a Christian. The first is the name of an office undertaken, the second a name of grace; that one means danger, this one salvation. Finally, as if in the open sea, I am being tossed about by the stormy activity involved in that one; but as I recall by whose blood I have been redeemed, I enter a safe harbour in the tranquil recollection of this one; and thus while toiling away at my own proper office, I take my rest in the marvellous benefit conferred on all of us in common. (Augustine, *Sermon 340,* in Edmund Hill, *Augustine, Sermons III/9 (306-340A) on the Saints* (Hyde Park: New City Press, 1994), p. 292).

Augustine was terrified of the fact that God had called him to be a bishop both because he was aware of the enormous importance of the bishop's role and of his inability, as a sinner, to undertake it in anything except an imperfect manner, and because he was aware that he would have to give account to God for his stewardship at the last judgement. What comforts him in the midst of his terror, he says in sermon 340, is the recollection that, just like the members of his flock, he is a Christian who has received the 'marvellous benefit' of the forgiveness of sins because of the saving work of Jesus Christ.

from those who would lead them astray in terms of belief or behaviour, and recover them when they have gone astray.

Secondly, they need to be guardians of the Christian faith as revealed in Holy Scripture and witnessed to by the writings of the Patristic period and the historic Anglican formularies. As guardians they need to point people to these sources of Christian truth, use them as the basis for their own teaching and practice, and do whatever they can to ensure that those ministers under their jurisdiction do the same.

Being a guardian of the faith in this way is not in tension with the idea that bishops are to be theological explorers. Everyone starts from somewhere in their quest for a deeper understanding of truth and the starting point for bishops is the faith of which they are the guardians.

Thirdly, they need to teach and preach. This is the heart of what bishops are called to do. They are called to feed the sheep themselves and cannot simply leave this role to others. Furthermore, their teaching and preaching needs to have a definite content and this content needs to be the faith of which they are the guardians. In addition, they need to know how to apply the truths of the Christian faith to the particular situations their flocks are facing, and they need to have the ability to act as apologists, able to commend and defend the faith to those outside the flock.

Fourthly, they need to be able to provide examples of holy living in their personal lives so that what they teach and preach is supported rather than undermined by how they behave.

Fifthly, in order to protect and recover the sheep, they need to combat error and exercise discipline. This means discerning and combatting doctrinal error and disciplining those ministers who teach it. It also means using the disciplinary tools available to them to exercise the power of the keys to both discipline and restore those members of the clergy who have erred in their behaviour.

Sixthly, they need to lead worship and preside over the celebration of the sacraments. When leading worship, they need to make sure that the form of worship conforms to church law, that the language of worship will be accessible to those who are present and that the content of worship will include the key elements of the reading and exposition of Scripture, a creedal affirmation of faith, the praise of God, the confession and absolution of sins, and intercessions. They will also need to be diligent in taking confirmation and in seeking to ensure that those in their dioceses understand the meaning of Baptism, Holy Communion and Confirmation and the responsibilities they involve.

Seventhly, they need to be leaders in mission. This means that they fulfil the five marks of mission themselves and teach, exhort and support others to do the same.

Eighthly, they need to promote unity in the Church. They cannot do this simply by being bishops in historic succession, or by being bishops to people of all shades of opinion are happy to relate to, but by helping God's people grow into the unity referred to by Paul in Ephesians 4:13, 'the unity of the faith and of the knowledge of the Son of God,' by undertaking the activities previously listed.

Ninthly, they need to ordain and appoint ministers, other shepherds to help care for the sheep. In specific terms this means that working with their fellow bishops and with others in the Church they need to ensure that there is a supply of ordained and lay ministers who understand and believe the Christian faith as the Church of England has received it, who are able to provide examples of godly living, and who have shown that they are willing and competent to teach and preach, to lead worship and preside at the sacraments, to correct error, to rebuke sin, and to restore the penitent.

Tenthly, they need to oversee the creation and maintenance of church buildings and churchyards in accordance with the laws of the Church and the state so that there are buildings in good order that can be used as places for worship and bases for mission and so that there are places where the bodies of the dead can be reverently laid to rest and where nature can be encouraged to flourish.

Eleventhly, they need to work with others in a collegial and communal fashion, but they cannot use this as an excuse to avoid their own personal responsibilities, and like Athanasius they need to be prepared to stand up against others for the sake of Christian truth and to use their powers of veto when it is necessary to do so.

Twelfthly, they need to keep on top of the administration which is an unavoidable part of being a bishop and when necessary, they need to be willing to accept help from others on their staff in order do to this.

In the light of this role description for a good-enough bishop, those selected to be bishops should be:

- People who are committed followers of Jesus Christ.
- People who are baptised and confirmed.
- People who understand and whole-heartedly assent to the Christian faith as set out in the Scriptures and witnessed to by the Creeds and other Patristic writings and by the Church of England's historic formularies.
- People whose personal and family lives model Christian holiness.

- People who have shown their ability to undertake the various aspects of the bishop's role during an extensive period serving as deacons and priests.
- People who have shown that they are prepared to work with others, but also prepared to stand firm against others for the sake of Christian truth when it is necessary to do so.
- People who have shown that they can keep on top of administration.

What is not necessary, however, is that they should have higher degrees in theology or qualifications in business administration. These may be helpful, but they are not necessary.

'Not good-enough' bishops

There are three categories of not good-enough bishops.

First, there are those who sincerely want to be good-enough bishops but are simply not up to the job. Ten reasons can be identified as to why this may be the case:

1) They could have only a superficial understanding of the Christian faith.
2) They could have a deep understanding of the Christian faith, but a poor understanding of the contemporary world.
3) They could have a lack of pastoral knowledge and experience.
4) They could have a deep understanding of both the Christian faith and the contemporary world and have practical knowledge of the cure of souls, but not be able to communicate effectively to either groups or individuals because of a lack of training or natural incapacity.
5) They could be poor at leading worship.
6) They could be a poor judge of people and therefore make poor appointments or continue to hold positions for which they are unsuited.
7) They could be bad at working with others.
8) They could be bad at handling conflict, either because they handle it in a way which causes

serious and lasting damage or because they seek to avoid at all costs it even when it is necessary.

9) They could be unable to keep on top of administration.

10) They could be incapable of getting the right balance between their primary diocesan commitment and work outside the diocese.

Secondly, there are what Augustine called 'bad bishops,'[9] those who want the benefits of being a bishop, but who have no intention of fulfilling the obligation that the office brings with it to be a faithful shepherd to a part of God's flock and an example of holy living.

Archbishop Lancelot Blackburne (Bishop of Exeter from 1717-1724 and Archbishop of York from 1724-1743) and Bishop Peter Ball (who was suffragan Bishop of Lewes from 1977-1992 and Bishop of Gloucester from 1992-1993) are examples of such 'bad bishops.' Blackburne almost totally neglected his episcopal duties and was also guilty of open sexual immorality, but at least he did not pretend to be godly. Ball's example is arguably even more heinous in that he used a carefully cultivated reputation for personal holiness as the founder of the new monastic community of The Glorious Ascension, and the position he had as a bishop, to give him the opportunity to fulfil his desire

---

[9] Augustine, *Sermon 340 A*: 6 in Hill (ed.) p. 300.

to engage in sexual activity with young men, as a result which he was eventually sent to prison.

Thirdly, there are those who propagate heresy in relation to Christian belief or behaviour. In the Patristic period Bishop Apollinarius of Laodicea and Patriarch Nestorius of Constantinople are examples of heretical bishops. Both developed Christological heresies, with the former teaching that that Christ had a body and soul but lacked a rational human mind (which was replaced by the divine Word) and the latter held that Christ was made up of two separate persons, the divine Son of God with his divine nature, and the human person Jesus with his human nature. In recent times Bishop Ernest Barnes (Bishop of Birmingham from 1924 – 1952), Bishop John Robinson (Suffragan bishop of Woolwich from 1959-1969) and Bishop Michael Ingham (Bishop of the Canadian diocese of New Westminster from 1994-2013) sought to adapt Christian doctrine and sexual ethics to fit in with the thinking of the modern world and in so doing departed from the teaching of the New Testament and the orthodox Christian theological tradition.

The reason that episcopal heresy has to be regarded as an extremely serious matter is because of the truth highlighted by the Athanasian Creed that salvation involves holding fast to the Catholic (i.e. orthodox) faith in both belief and behaviour and heresy and that heresy therefore brings with it the risk of the ultimate spiritual harm of eternal damnation. Bishops who are heretics are thus putting at harm the flocks they are meant to protect.

The correct approach to the first category of 'not good-enough bishops,' is for people to pray for the bishop concerned and work with him or her to help them become good-enough. If in the long term it becomes apparent that this is not going to happen the bishop should be encouraged to resign or retire with as much dignity and support as possible so that a bishop who will be good-enough can then be appointed.

With the second and third categories, the teaching of Article XXVI comes into play. This means that the episcopal acts of bad or heretical bishops (such as confirmation or ordination) should be regarded as valid, but that nevertheless that it is necessary for faithful Christians to contend against the ungodliness of ungodly bishops and the heresy of heretical ones, using the *Clergy Discipline Measure* and the *Ecclesiastical Jurisdiction Measure* to try to depose bishops from office if they are not willing to repent and change their behaviour, their teaching, or their heretical practice.

In addition:

(a) Christians should avoid any feeling of moral superiority over not good-enough bishops.

(b) They should contend against heresy in a godly way, treating those involved in heresy with dignity and respect.

(c) If heretical bishops remain in office, faithful Christians need to seek some form of alternative episcopal oversight and in this situation orthodox bishops should be prepared to follow Patristic precedent by offering such oversight outside the bounds of their normal jurisdiction.

For a more detailed account of what is said in this chapter see chapters 14-15 of *Bishops Past, Present and Future.*

3. THE CHALLENGES FACING BISHOPS TODAY BECAUSE OF THE SECULARISATION OF WESTERN SOCIETY

Church of England bishops today face a range of specific local challenges that are much the same as the problems that other bishops have faced during the history of the Church. Such challenges are, for instance, the existence of difficult working relationships, clergy and laity going off the rails, a lack of resources and excessive demands on the bishop's time.

They also face the challenge of helping people both inside and outside the Church to deal with the multiple social problems facing Britain today including, for example, the continuing effects of Covid-19, the rising cost of living, lack of affordable housing, and the existence of modern forms of slavery.

However, in addition to these specific challenges, there is one overarching challenge which is new and which all bishops (and indeed all Christians) now face, which is how to respond to the dominance of a secular ideology in Western society and the potential effects of this ideology on the life of the Church both now and in the years to come.

How the dominant secular ideology has developed[10]

Carl Trueman's important study *The Rise and Triumph of the Modern Self* addresses the question of why it is that in contemporary Western society it has come to be regarded as meaningful to say 'I am a woman trapped in a man's body' (and unacceptable to question this statement) when previous generations would have dismissed this statement as completely absurd.

Trueman's answer to this question is that the reason the statement is now regarded as meaningful is because a number of interrelated developments that have taken place across the Western world since the second half of the eighteenth century have together led to a radical shift in what Trueman calls the 'social imaginary'—that is, the way most people understand the world and how to behave within it.[11]

These developments have been as follows:

First, the secularisation of Western society and the consequent loss of the sense of the world as God's creation means that there has been a shift in people's views of the world from *mimesis* (from the Greek for

---

[10] The paragraphs that follow are adapted from Martin Davie, *Living in Love and Faith – A Biblical Response* (Oxford: Dictum Press, 2021), pp. 83-89.
[11] Carl Trueman, *The Rise and Triumph of the Modern Self* (Wheaton: Crossway, 2020), pp. 36-37.

'imitation') to *poesis* (meaning 'creating). As Trueman explains:

> A *mimetic* view regards the world as having a given order and a given meaning and thus sees human beings as required to discover that meaning and conform themselves to it. *Poiesis*, by way of contrast, sees the world as so much raw material out of which meaning and purpose can be created by the individual.[12]

Secondly, there has been the related loss of the idea of 'sacred order'. In Western culture today most people no longer believe that there is fixed moral order which has been established by God and which all human beings therefore need to respect.

Thirdly, as a result, Western culture lacks an agreed basis for ethics. So, as Alasdair MacIntyre has argued, the basis of ethical decision-making has, by default, become mere emotivism—that is, ethics based on personal feeling and preference.[13]

Fourthly, there has also been a change in the way in which most people view the purpose of human existence—the good to which human beings should aspire. What has emerged is what Charles Taylor calls a 'culture of authenticity'. This is an understanding of life that says

---

[12] Trueman, p. 39.
[13] Alasdair MacIntyre, *After Virtue* (London: Duckworth, 1983).

... that each of us has his/her own way of realizing our humanity, and that it is important to find and live out one's own way—as against surrendering to conformity with a model imposed on us from outside, by society, or by the previous generation, or religious or political authority.'[14]

Fifthly, there has been the development of what Philip Rieff calls the 'therapeutic society'—a society in which social institutions are viewed as being set up to foster the individual's sense of psychological well-being as they live out their unique authentic existence.[15]

Sixthly, since the work of Sigmund Freud, it has come to be widely believed that 'humans, from infancy onward, are at core sexual beings. It is our sexual desires that are ultimately decisive for who we are.'[16] The acceptance of Freud's ideas has been facilitated by the huge growth in pornography but also the many developments in modern medicine which make the results of sexual activity less serious by separating sex from childbirth and by providing more effective treatment for sexually-transmitted diseases.

Finally, the work of Neo-Marxist scholars such as Wilhelm Reich and Herbert Marcuse has led to the idea

---

[14] Charles Taylor, *A Secular Age* (Cambridge Ma and London: Belknapp Press, 2007), p. 475.
[15] See Philip Rieff, *The Triumph of the Therapeutic* (Chicago: Chicago University Press, 1966).
[16] Trueman, p. 27.

that the traditional view of the family (consisting of a married couple and their children), together with the traditional sexual morality linked to this, are inherently oppressive and need to be overthrown.

Imaginary identity and subjective experience

As Trueman argues, the result of these seven developments has been to create a 'social imaginary' that is based on *poiesis* rather than *mimesis*: we live in a world of our creating. In such a world the idea of being a woman trapped in a man's body begins to make sense. On the one hand, there is no fixed order of things, and no fixed pattern for human existence or behaviour; thus there is no yardstick against which one can measure whether the idea is wrong. On the other, it becomes perfectly natural for an individual to say something such as:

> 'The purpose of my existence is to live as authentically as possible in accordance with what I perceive to be my true self. If this then involves seeing myself as a woman, even though I have a man's body, then that is what I should do.
>
> Furthermore, society should support me in so doing because only then will I achieve psychological well-being. Thinking otherwise is immoral because it involves damaging my psychological well-being through a refusal to give recognition to who I believe myself to be.'

The same factors create a social imaginary in which the acceptance of same-sex relationships and the claim to a gay or lesbian identity also makes sense. Again, there is no fixed order of things and no fixed pattern for human behaviour, and thus no yardstick against which one can say same-sex relationships are wrong. And so, the individual may often justify an action as follows:

'The purpose of my existence is to live as authentically as possible in accordance with what I perceive to be my true self. If this involves having sex with someone of my own sex, then that is what I should do. In addition, because, as Freud has taught us, sexual desire is at the core of human identity, my desire for sex with someone of my own sex defines who I am. I *am* gay or lesbian.'

As Trueman goes on to say, within this worldview:

'...mere tolerance of homosexuality is bound to become unacceptable. The issue is not one of simply decriminalizing behaviour; that would certainly mean that homosexual acts were tolerated by society, but the acts are only part of the overall problem. The real issue is one of recognition, of recognizing the legitimacy of who the person thinks he actually is. This requires more than mere tolerance, it requires equality before the law and recognition by the law and in society. And that means that those who refuse to grant such recognition will be the ones who find themselves on the wrong side of both the law and emerging social attitudes.

The person who objects to homosexual practice is, in contemporary society, actually objecting to homosexual identity. And the refusal by any individual to recognize an identity that society at large recognizes as legitimate is a moral offense, not simply a matter of indifference.'[17]

This is why LGBTQI+ campaigners react so strongly against the idea that those Christians who object to same-sex sexual relationships can speak of 'hating the sin but loving the sinner'. Within a post-Freudian worldview sexual identity and sexual behaviour cannot be separated. Hence to hate the sin is also to hate the sinner.

An additional but related aspect of modern Western culture is the central place given to personal experience. If there is no fixed moral order, how should individuals decide how they should live? The answer increasingly is that they should simply 'try it and see'. In other words, as they proceed through life they should decide, on the basis of their personal experience, what pattern of life, and what pattern of sexual identity and activity, gives them that sense of psychological well-being which is the proper goal of life.

As Trueman points out,[18] this idea of experience as normative can be found in one of the seminal works of

---

[17] Trueman, pp. 68-69.
[18] Trueman, Chapter 3.

modern Western thought, Jean-Jacques Rousseau *Confessions.*[19] Life, according to Rousseau, should be lived on the basis of reflecting on one's experience. This approach stands in contrast to the earlier *Confessions* of Augustine.[20] For Augustine what is normative is not his experiences, but the teaching of Scripture, since it is only through the witness of Scripture that he is able to make sense of his experiences.

What all this means is that Western society has now reached a place where human beings are playing the role of their own creator, constructing identities for themselves, and testing everything at the solitary bar of their own subjective experience. I am who I think I am on the basis of my unique experience and everybody else must accept this fact.

Western secular ideology from a Christian perspective

From a Christian perspective there are three fundamental problems with the Western secular ideology described by Trueman.

The first problem is that it is idolatrous. It is idolatrous because it puts human beings in the place of the creator God. It falsely claims that it is we and not God who create who we are and who determine how we should live. It is also idolatrous because it sees the highest human good as being not to love and serve God, but to

---

[19] Jean-Jacques Rousseau, *Confessions* (Oxford: OUP, 2008).

[20] Augustine, *The Confessions* (Oxford: OUP, 2008).

love and serve our own subjective desires, particularly our desire for sexual fulfilment.

The second problem is that it insists that everybody has to accept the claims I make about my own identity. This idea is problematic because it assumes that I can never be mistaken about who I am. However, the fact that humans can be (and frequently are) mistaken means that it actually makes perfectly good sense for someone who has, or thinks they have, better information about who I am than I have, to refuse to accept my account of myself.

This further means that there is nothing wrong in principle with Christians believing that those who identify as gay, or lesbian were not created to find their fulfilment in sexual relations with those of the same-sex, or with Christians declining to accept that someone who is biologically male is actually female, or vice-versa.

The third problem is that it mistakenly contrasts obedience to God's will as revealed in Scripture and the Christian tradition with the exercise of human freedom. As Richard Bauckham explains:

> The crux is the question of obedience to God's will. Is this a kind of heteronomy (subjection to another) that contradicts human autonomy (self-determination)? Many modern people think so. But, properly understood, obedience to God transcends this contradiction. When I love God and freely make God's will my own, I am not forfeiting my freedom but fulfilling it.

God's will is not the will of another in any ordinary sense. It is the moral truth of all reality. To conform ourselves freely to that truth is also to conform to the inner law of our own created being. To learn obedience to God involves, of course, a long and painful struggle, as it did for Jesus (Hebrews 5:8), who exercised his freedom as Son never more fully that in his acceptance off his Father's will in Gethsemane (Mark 14:36). But it is a journey into the fullest freedom: the goal of our salvation in which theonomy (obedience to God's will) and autonomy will fully coincide. That is why the Anglican collect for peace says that 'to serve you is perfect freedom.'

Once again, the key is love. The limit constituted by God's will is not a restriction on our freedom when we accept it by loving God by freely embracing God's will, by making God's will our own. We transcended the limit by accepting it. In this way we fulfil through love of God the freedom we receive from God through God's love for us.[21]

Two further challenges

The fundamental challenge that the existence of this ideology poses for the Church in the Western World, is that it means that the Church now exists in a society in

---

[21] Richard Bauckham, *God and the Crisis of Freedom* (Louisville: Westminster John Knox Press, 2002), pp. 46-47.

which the majority of people view the world through the lens of an aggressive and all-pervasive ideology that is problematic for the three reasons just described. Like the Church of the first three centuries, or the Church in Eastern Europe during the Communist era, the Church in the Western World, including the Church of England, has to be willing to be counter cultural by maintaining and proclaiming Christian truth in a world that is dominated by lies.[22] The challenge for bishops is how to lead the Church in doing this.

This challenge is made more difficult by the fact that the influence of the ideology that has just been described has resulted in two further challenges to the Christian Church in the Western World (including the Church of England), one external and one internal.

Being the bad guys

The external challenge has two elements to it. The first element is that for very many in the Western world the incompatibility between traditional Christian theology and sexual ethics and the modern belief in self-creation and sexual freedom means that Christians are now the 'bad guys.'

To quote Stewart McAlpine:

> Only a few generations ago, Christianity was the good guy, the solution to what was bad. Rather than being on the wrong side of the law,

---

[22] For this point see Rod Dreher, *Live Not by Lies – A Manual for Christian Dissenters* (New York: Sentinel, 2020).

we were the law. Christian morality was assumed and passed mainly unchallenged. The cultural, legal and political power structures affirmed Christians. Then something changed. Over the course of the twentieth century, we became just one of the guys: one option among many - a voice to be considered but not to be followed unquestioningly. If Christianity worked for you, fine; if it didn't work for me, also fine.

Most of us think we still live in that world. Most Christian books, sermons and podcasts assume that we do. In many ways, we've only just worked out how to live well as one of the guys.

But the problem is that that's not where we are now. The tide has shifted further. Christianity is no longer an option; it's a problem. The cultural, political and legal guns that Christianity once held are now trained on us - and it's happened quickly. The number of those professing faith has fallen dramatically. The number of those who reject the faith they held until their late teens has risen dramatically. The seat at the cultural table that we assumed was ours for keeps is increasingly being given to others. We're on the wrong side of history, the wrong side of so many issues and conversations. If this were a Western, we would be the guys wearing the black hats whose appearance is accompanied by the foreboding soundtrack. It's come as a surprise, we're not

sure how it happened, we don't like it and we
don't feel we deserve it - but we are the bad guys
now. [23]

The perception that Christians are the bad guys and
that their sexual ethics are morally unacceptable has
been reinforced in recent years by the revelation of
cases of sexual abuse in numerous churches, such as
the sexual abuse perpetrated by Bishop Peter Ball noted
earlier in this study. The existence of such abuse is seen
as somehow discrediting further Christian ethical
teaching even though the abuse in question happened
precisely because the abusers deliberately disregarded
Christian sexual ethics in the way they behaved.

Because Christians are now the bad guys, and because
people need protection from the bad guys, the second
element of the external challenge is that Christians are
now increasingly facing not only widespread social
disapproval, but the threat of legal sanctions against
what have hitherto been viewed as perfectly normal
forms of religious activity.

For example, as George Hobson writes:

Critics of homosexual practice and the gay
lifestyle, even when they are welcoming of gays
and eager to help those who wish to change
their lifestyle, are labelled 'homophobic' and
are subject to the severest condemnation by
those who see themselves as morally

---

[23] Stewart McAlpine, *Being the Bay Guys – How to live for
Jesus in a world that says you shouldn't* (Epsom: The Good
Book Company 2021), kindle edition, pp. 2-3.

enlightened. On account of the politicization of this issue through pressure from the powerful Gay Lobby and its political supporters, it will soon become a criminal offence to offer such criticism, and Christian organizations such as churches or Christian schools that cleave to traditional biblically based ethical doctrine and practice will come under attack in the courts and even find their leaders being dragged off to jail. [24]

Although Hobson is writing specifically about the response to criticism of homosexual practice, the same sort of response is also now made to those who are critical of the practice of gender transition. They too now face severe moral condemnation as transphobic and the threat of legal sanctions.

This two-part external challenge creates two problems for the Church. First, the perception of Christians as

---

[24] George Hobson, The Episcopal Church, Homosexuality and the Context of Technology, (Eugene: Pickwick Publications, 2013), kindle edition, Loc.3114-3124. The current trial of a Christian MP and a Lutheran bishop in Finland for publishing material expressing a traditional Christian sexual ethic ('Trial of Räsänen and Pohjola completed: decision comes at the end of March' https://evangelicalfocus.com/europe/15454/trial-of-rasanen-and-pohjola-completed-decision-comes-at-the-end-of-march) and the calls in the UK for a ban on 'conversion therapy' that would effectively outlaw many forms of Christian ministry including simply praying with people (see 'Let us pray' at https://letuspray.uk/) are evidence of the truth of Hobson's statement.

the 'bad guys' makes it more difficult for the Christian message to get a hearing. After all, who wants to listen to what the bad guys have to say? If Christians are 'homophobes' and 'transphobes' then the rest of what they have to say can simply be dismissed. Secondly, the perception that Christians are 'bad guys' and the threat of legal action against those who espouse traditional Christian doctrine and practice will inhibit the Church's work in that it will lead people to refuse to publish Christian material, lead to Christians having restricted access to the media, and mean that organisations will refuse to let Christians use their venues for meetings. In addition, it will potentially mean Christians having to choose between disobeying God or suffering punishment for breaking the law, neither of which is desirable.

Rejecting a theology of unconditional affirmation and cheap grace

The internal challenge to the Church is posed by a new form of theology that first became prevalent in North America but has now spread across the Western world. As Philip Turner explains in his essay 'ECUSA's God and the Idols of Liberal Protestantism', this theology begins with the belief that:

> .... the incarnation is to be understood (in an almost exhaustive sense) as a manifestation of divine love. From this starting point, several conclusions are drawn. The first is that God is love pure and simple. Thus, one is to see in Christ's death no judgement upon the human condition. Rather, one is to see an affirmation

of creation and the persons we are. The great news of the Christian gospel is this. God wants us to love one another, and such love requires of us both acceptance and affirmation of the other. From this point we can derive yet another, accepting love requires a form of justice that is inclusive of all people, particularly those who in some way have been marginalized by oppressive social practice. The mission of the church is therefore to see that those who have been rejected are included and that justice as inclusion defines public policy.[25]

As the title of Turner's essays reveals, in these words he is describing what he calls the 'working theology' of The Episcopal Church in the United States. However, as previously noted, this theology has spread across the Western world, and it has now firmly taken root in the Church of England. Thus, the mantra of the need for 'inclusion' which has spread across the Church of England in recent years reflects the influence of the sort of theology summarised by Turner.

It is not difficult to see the connection between this kind of theology and the prevailing cultural ethos of diversity, equality and inclusion which has resulted from the developments in Western culture described by Trueman. According to the diversity, equality and inclusion ethos, everyone is to be accepted and

---

[25] Philip Turner, 'ECUSA's God and the Idols of Liberal Protestantism' in Ephraim Radner and Philip Turner, *The Fate of Communion* (Grand Rapids and Cambridge: Eerdmans, 2006, p. 249).

affirmed on their own terms, particularly the members of hitherto marginalized sexual minorities. In similar fashion, in the theology described by Turner everyone is to be accepted and affirmed by those in Church because everyone is unconditionally affirmed and accepted by God.

Furthermore, just as in wider society acceptance and affirmation are seen as requiring the social inclusion of the members of sexual minorities on their own terms as a matter of justice, so within the Church (including in the Church of England) it is increasingly being argued that justice demands that members of sexual minorities are likewise fully accepted on their own terms, which in turn means that LGBT people should be able to serve in all forms of ministry and that churches should be willing to celebrate same-sex marriages.

For example, the 'The Change We Want to See' section of the website of the LGBT pressure group One Body One Faith declares:

- we want the Christian churches to be places where all people, particularly those who identify as gay, lesbian, bisexual or transgender, are welcomed and affirmed, not just tolerated.
- we want church communities to be places where people are safe to explore questions of sexuality, faith and spirituality in ways which are intelligent, respectful and compassionate,

where we can reach different conclusions without hurting one another.

- we want gay, lesbian, bisexual, and transgender people to be treated the same way as our straight and cisgendered siblings, in our lives, our relationships and our ministry.
- we want to be able to celebrate our marriages in our places of worship, so that we can acknowledge God as the source of the love between and within us.
- we want our families to feel welcome in our churches, throughout their journey of life and faith, and especially when they are feeling vulnerable or confused or facing times of transition and change.
- we want to be able to offer our gifts in all forms of ministry, on the same terms as our brothers and sisters, and not to have to choose between our calling to serve God, and our loving relationships.[26]

From this viewpoint it is not enough for churches to say that LGBT people are welcome to attend. To be properly inclusive churches must also fully accept their relationships (hence allowing same-sex marriages) and their gender identities and cease to place any restrictions on the ministries they are allowed to exercise.

---

[26] One Body One Faith, 'The Change We Went to See' at https://www.onebodyonefaith.org.uk/about-us/the-change-we-want-to-see/

From an orthodox Christian perspective, the underlying theology of unqualified divine love and affirmation on which this challenge is based is heretical for two reasons.

It is heretical because it claims that Christ's death involved no judgement on the human condition. This is heretical because if we ask why Christ had to die our death on the cross in order that we might be saved the answer Paul gives us in Romans 6: 6-7 is that:

> We know that our old self was crucified with him that the sinful body might be destroyed and we might no longer be enslaved to sin. For he who has died is freed from sin.

What he is saying in these verses is that our fallen nature was slain in the death of Christ in order that we might have liberation from the domination by sin which our old nature ('our old self') necessarily entails. Christ's death was thus *both* an act of God's judgement *and* an act of God's love. The cross was an act of God's judgement in that on the cross the death penalty was carried out on us as sinners. Our sinful existence ('the sinful body') has no right to exist before God and it was therefore ended. It was at the same time an act of love since the purpose of this judgement was to destroy our enslavement to sin in order that we might become free to be the people God intends us to be.

It is also heretical because it teaches what Dietrich Bonhoeffer famously labelled 'cheap grace', that is 'grace without repentance.'[27] It affirms God's love for us, but it is silent about our need to respond to that love in repentance.

As Hobson explains, the issue is that:

> God in Christ is turned towards us, yes: but we as sinners living in a fallen world are by nature turned in on ourselves and away from him, and we cannot authentically go toward him unless we first turn round, or change course, which is what repentance means. [28]

As he goes on to say:

> In order to receive the gift of forgiveness of sins, the promised gift of the Holy Spirit, and the gift of eternal life won for us by the atoning passion of Jesus Christ, we must repent and believe, and this will involve going in the opposite direction from the self-focused one we were travelling in before. The Bible calls this '*metanoia.*' It is a matter of conversion. Jesus becomes our Lord and Master instead of our own ego. The way we experience this turning away from self and towards God will vary greatly from person to person, but it must happen if we want to be incorporated genuinely into the 'new creation' that the authentic Church, as a corporate society, *is,* and that each

---

[27] Dietrich Bonhoeffer, *The Cost of Discipleship* (London: SCM, 1959) p. 35.
[28] Hobson, Loc.2933.

believer, as a member by faith of this corporate society , *is* (Galatians 6:15; 2 Corinthians 5:17; Ephesians 4:24). [29]

The truth that Christ's death was an act of judgement and the requirement for repentance go together because the character of repentance is to turn away from those things belonging to our sinful state which were put to death when Christ died on the cross. That is why the Christian life has traditionally been seen in terms of mortification and vivification, mortification involving the rejection of the old way of life which was put to death when Christ died for us, and vivification involving the entering into the new way of life that Christ died to make possible.

Furthermore, just as it is heretical to say that God simply loves and affirms us without acknowledging the reality of God's judgement and the need for repentance, so also it is heretical to say that the role of the Church is simply to accept and affirm people. This is because the Church is called to preach 'repentance and the forgiveness of sins' (Luke 24:47). That is to say, the Church must make clear to people the truth which we have just been outlining, namely that receiving the forgiveness of sins that Christ offers involves people being willing, in the power given to them by God through the Holy Spirit, to turn away from that sinful form of existence from which Christ died to set them free.

---

[29] Hobson, Loc. 2946-2965.

We can see Paul making just this point clear to the Christians in Galatia in Galatians 5:16-24:

> But I say, walk by the Spirit, and do not gratify the desires of the flesh. For the desires of the flesh are against the Spirit, and the desires of the Spirit are against the flesh; for these are opposed to each other, to prevent you from doing what you would. But if you are led by the Spirit you are not under the law. Now the works of the flesh are plain: fornication, impurity, licentiousness, idolatry, sorcery, enmity, strife, jealousy, anger, selfishness, dissension, party spirit, envy, drunkenness, carousing, and the like. I warn you, as I warned you before, that those who do such things shall not inherit the kingdom of God. But the fruit of the Spirit is love, joy, peace, patience, kindness, goodness, faithfulness, gentleness, self-control; against such there is no law. And those who belong to Christ Jesus have crucified the flesh with its passions and desires.

Finally, as has already been indicated in chapter 15, it would be heretical for a church to do what LGBT pressure groups such as One Body One Church demand, which is to accept and affirm LGBT people without requiring them to repent of same-sex sexual relationships or the assumption of a gender identity that does not reflect the sexual identity given to them by God. Rather than being an act of justice this would be an act of double *injustice*, injustice against God, by telling people that they do not have to live in the way

God created them to live, and injustice against the people concerned who would be left living in this way with the risk of being cut off from God and all good for ever.

To understand why this is so we must begin by recognising that when God created human beings in his image and likeness, he created them to be male or female. In the words of Genesis 1:27: 'So God created man in his own image, in the image of God he created him; male and female he created them.' This teaching is reiterated by Jesus in Matthew 19:4: 'Have you not read that he who made them from the beginning made them male and female.'

There is a very small percentage of people, some 0.018% of live births (approximately 1:500), who are genuinely 'intersex' in the sense that they combine both male and female elements in their physiology. However, the existence of such people still points to the fundamentally dimorphic, male or female, nature of human sexuality. Where they are able to reproduce, and that is often not the case, they do so either as male or female. Their condition is a developmental disorder rather than the existence of a third type of human being and is the exception that proves the rule.

Because this is the case, except in these highly exceptional and biologically distinct cases, believing rightly in 'God the Father who hath made me and all the world' in the words of the Prayer Book Catechism, means accepting with gratitude that I am the particular male or female human being that God has created me to be and living accordingly.

As Oliver O'Donovan writes in his book *Begotten or Made?*:

> When God made mankind male and female, to exist alongside each other and for each other, he gave a form that human sexuality should take and a good to which it should aspire. None of us can, or should, regard our difficulties with that form, or with achieving that good, as the norm of what our sexuality is to be. None of us should see our sexuality as mere self-expression, and forget that we can express ourselves sexually only because we participate in this generic form and aspire to this generic good. We do not have to make a sexual form, or posit a sexual good. We have to exist as well as we can within that sexual form, and in relation to that sexual good, which has been given to us because it has been given to humankind.[30]

This means that it is not legitimate either to deny the God-given form by rejecting the division of humanity into male and female, or to deny the particular version of that form that God has given to us by making us either male or female, something that is determined not by our feelings (as many today would claim), but by

---

[30] Oliver O'Donovan, *Begotten or Made?* (Oxford: OUP, 1984), pp. 28-29.

our biology. As we have noted before, 'my body is me' and this means that 'my biology is me.'

However difficult the form that God has given us may be for us to accept, to deny it would be sinful because it would involve refusing to say to God 'thy will be done' by refusing to love the self who God has made us to be.

Refusing in this way to say to God 'thy will be done,' in either our thinking or our behaviour, is a very serious matter because it brings with it the inescapable risk of eternal separation from God. As C S Lewis writes in his book *The Great Divorce*, there is an inescapable binary choice facing all human beings. 'There are only two kinds of people in the end: those who say to God, 'Thy will be done,' and those to whom God says, in the end, 'Thy will be done.'' [31]

Lewis' point is that God has given human beings freedom to shape their own destinies. We can choose to say to God 'thy will be done' and be happy with God for ever in the world to come, or we can choose to turn our back on God. If we do this God will respect our decision, but the inevitable consequence will be that in the world to come we will be cut off from God and all good for ever. The fundamental problem with both gender transition and same-sex relationships is that they do involve a rejection, in both theory and practice, of the sexual identity which we have been given by God and thus a failure to say to God 'thy will be done.'

---

[31] C S Lewis, *The Great Divorce* (Glasgow: Fontana, 1972), pp. 66-67.

Gender transition

In the case of gender transition, the issue is people who are suffering from a deep discomfort with their sexual identity (the condition known as 'gender dysphoria') refusing to accept the sexual identity of their body as given and seeking some to inhabit some other form of sexual identity instead. By doing this they act in a way that is incompatible with the biblical teaching that we should live in accordance with the sexual identity that God has given to us by the creation of the particular bodies that we possess.

This teaching can be found in Deuteronomy 22:5 which prohibits cross-dressing on the grounds that, as Peter Harland puts it: 'to dress after the manner of the opposite sex was to infringe the normal order of creation which divided humanity into male and female.'[32] It can also be found in 1 Corinthians 11:2-16 where St Paul tells the Corinthians that men should follow the dress and hair codes which proclaim them to be male and women the codes which proclaim them to be female because, in the words of Tom Wright in his commentary on this verse: 'God's creation needs humans to be fully, gloriously and truly human, which means fully and truly male and female'.[33]

---

[32] P.J. Harland 'Menswear and Womenswear: A Study of Deuteronomy 22:5,' (*Expository Times,* 110, No.3, 1988), p. 76.
[33] Tom Wright, *Paul for Everyone – I Corinthians* (London: SPCK, 2003), p. 143.

Such teaching does not mean that Christians should uncritically embrace the gender stereotypes of any given society. What it does mean is that we should glorify God through our bodies by living in a way that proclaims to our society the truth of our creation by God as male or female. We should be saying through our bodies, God has made me male, or God has made me female.

Engaging in gender transition is incompatible with this calling because it necessarily involves refusing to accept and live out the truth of the male or female identity that God the creator has given to us, by deliberately adopting instead an artificially created alternate identity instead. To acknowledge this point is not to minimise the acute distress experienced by people with gender dysphoria. It is, rather, to give a theological account of what using gender transition to relieve this distress entails.

The argument is often made that people who engage in gender transition cannot be said to be sinning since they are not deliberately choosing to go against God's will. They see the identity they are seeking to live out as their true God given identity, their 'authentic self,' and they simply desire to live according to this true identity.

This argument is true as an account of how the people involved view their situation. However, two further points need to be noted.

First, we have to distinguish between how an individual subjectively views their identity and what is objectively true. To be male or female is a matter of biology, it is a matter of the body someone has been given by God and for which and in which they are called to glorify him, and this truth is unaffected by how someone views him or herself. This means that someone who is biologically male or female, and who rejects this identity, is in fact rejecting the sex that God has given them, regardless of how they themselves view the matter.

Secondly, the fact that people with gender dysphoria have a distorted view of their situation which they then make the basis of sinful actions is not in fact something which makes them unique. As a result of the Fall human beings have lost the ability to always see things as they truly are (see Romans 1:21). Acts of sin (of whatever kind) occur when a distorted view of reality resulting from the Fall leads to wrong desires which in turn give birth to wrong actions. As Augustine argues in Book XIV of The City of God, 'our will is for our welfare' and this results in acts of sin because, misled in our thinking as a result of the Fall, 'we commit sin to promote our welfare.'[34] This is what is involved in gender transition just as in all other forms of sin. Eve wanted the apple because she thought it would be for her good. People desire gender transition for the same reason.

Same-sex relationships

In the case of same-sex relationships the rejection of sexual identity, and hence the rejection of the body,

---

[34] Augustine, *The City of God*, Book XIV.4, text in David Knowles (ed), Augustine, City of God (Harmondsworth: Penguin 1972), p. 553.

may appear to be less obvious, but it still exists. The point is that same-sex relationships involve either a man refusing to accept that as a man he was created by God to have sex with a woman: or a woman refusing to accept that as woman she was created to have sex with a man.

This does not, of course, mean that to be a man or a woman one has to have sex with a member of the opposite sex. Christ and John the Baptist were no less male and no less fully human for being celibate. What it does mean is that a man was created to have sex with a woman rather than a man (and vice versa). To be a man is to be one who is potentially husband-to-a-wife, father-to-a-child and vice versa. To engage in same-sex sexual activity is to reject this God given truth about human sexual identity. It is very similar to gender transition in that it rejects a core aspect of the duty to conform our lifestyle and behaviour to the form of embodiment that God has given us.

As O'Donovan writes, human beings are:

> ... clearly ordered at the biological level towards heterosexual union as the human mode of procreation. It is not possible to negotiate this fact about our common humanity; it can only be either welcomed or resented.[35]

To engage in same-sex activity is sinful because it involves translating resentment against the way we

---

[35] Oliver O'Donovan, *Transsexualism – Issues and Argument* (Cambridge: Grove Books, 2007), p. 6.

have been made by God into a form of activity which actively goes against the way God has made us to be. It involves saying 'I will live the way I want to live regardless of the way God made me.' This may not be what people consciously think they are doing, but it is what they are doing in practice.

This is the point that underlies the prohibition of sexual relationships between men in Leviticus 18:22 and 20:13. Like all the other sexual prohibitions in these two chapters, the prohibition of men having sex with other men reflects the teaching contained in Genesis 1 and 2 about how God created the world. According to this teaching, God created human beings as male and female, with men designed to have sexual relations with women within marriage and vice versa. Gay sex is an 'abomination' in Leviticus because it involves a rejection by an individual of this key aspect of the created order.

This is also the point that Paul is making when he describes same-sex relationships as 'unnatural' (*para phusin*) in Romans 1:27. In line with other Jewish thinkers of his time, Paul thinks they are unnatural because they violate the heterosexual form of sexual activity God has created men and women to engage in (as shown by the way their bodies are constructed).

For Paul same-sex sexual activity is thus a rejection of human createdness which parallels, and points to, the rejection of the creator through idolatry. That is why he cites it as the first example of the consequences of idolatry in human behaviour. As Tom Wright puts it 'the fact that such clear distortions of the creator's male-plus-female intention occur in the world indicates that the human race as a whole is guilty of a character-twisting idolatry'.[36] Rejecting the creator and rejecting our createdness go together.

Same-sex marriages are a further development of the basic error involved in all same-sex relationships. In terms of Christian theology, they too involve a failure to conform our sexual relationships to our God given embodiment. Marriage as created by God is a sexual relationship between two people of the opposite sex (Genesis 2:18-24). It follows that two men cannot enter into marriage with each other, and neither can two women. Same-sex marriages involve a denial of this truth.

What all this means is that same-sex relationships (including same-sex marriages) and gender transition both involve a rejection of the necessary implications of the first article of the Creed. People may still sincerely believe in 'God the Father Almighty, Maker of heaven and earth,' but they refuse to truly accept, or live out, this belief in so far as it relates to the existence of the particular men and women whom God has created.

As Martin Luther explains in his *Small Catechism*, the answer to the question of what it means to confess 'I

---

[36] Tom Wright, *Paul for Everyone, Romans, Part 1: Chapters 1-8* (London: SPCK, 2004), pp.22-23. For a detailed exploration of Paul's teaching in Romans 1 see Robert Gagnon, *The Bible and Homosexual Practice* (Nashville: Abingdon Press, 2001), pp. 229-302.

believe in God, the Father almighty, Maker of heaven and earth' is 'I believe that God has created me and all that exists; that he has given me and still sustains my body and soul, all my limbs and senses, my reason and all the faculties of my mind'. In other words, the Christian belief in God the creator is not just a vague deistic belief that God is the ultimate source of all that is, but also the very specific belief testified to in Psalm 139 that God made me as the particular combination of body and soul that I am. Both same-sex relationships and gender transition involve in different ways a rejection of that basic truth. They thus involve, ultimately, a failure to say to God 'thy will be done' and to glorify God in the body by living according to this truth, and this, as previously noted, carries the risk of eternal damnation. That is why Paul warns the Corinthians in 1 Corinthians 6:10 that those who persist in same-sex sexual activity 'will not inherit the kingdom of God.'

Because this is the case, from an orthodox Christian perspective any church which supports same-sex relationships or gender transition is a church which is in serious error in its teaching and practice. It is giving support to forms of behaviour which involve serious moral error because they involve people departing from the way God created them to live. To put it simply, it is a church which does not love people enough to seek to prevent them from living in ways that are contrary to way God made them to live.

Love does not mean simply affirming whatever choices people wish to make. It means seeking their ultimate good by helping them to understand what the right choices are and then helping them to choose them. A church which gives support to same-sex relationships or gender transition is failing to do this.

4. BACK TO THE FUTURE: HOW BISHOPS SHOULD MEET THE CHALLENGES OF OUR DAY

Why the early Church triumphed

As has already been noted, the Church today is back in the situation it was in the early centuries. Then too it faced a society marked by an idolatrous world view and a lax view of sexual ethics, in which Christians were widely regarded as the 'bad guys' and in which faithful Christians faced legal penalties including, on occasion, the death penalty.

The good news is that the Church of the early centuries eventually triumphed. In spite of the opposition it faced, the Church thrived and grew, with scholars estimating that it grew by about 40% in the decade up to the end of the 4th century. Contrary to what has often been suggested it did not triumph because it was recognised by Constantine. It was already triumphing by the time Constantine recognised it.

If we ask why the Early Church triumphed in this way the fundamental theological answer is, of course, that God made it happen. However, as the Westminster Confession reminds us, in his providential work in the world 'God maketh use of means'[37] to carry out his purposes and in the case of the Early Church the

---

[37] *The Westminster Confession* V.II in Leith p. 200.

'means' that God used was a church that had seven key characteristics.

First, *it was a church that had a clear structure of theological authority.* The ultimate authority was the Scriptures, but alongside the Scriptures there was the 'rule of faith' (the precursor of the Creeds) that summarised the key teaching of the Scriptures and provided a framework for interpreting them correctly. In addition, as we have seen, it had in the bishops a set of people whose primary responsibility it was to teach the Scriptures, as interpreted according to the rule of faith, and to make sure that other members of the clergy did the same.

Secondly, *it was a church that sought to make sure that the teaching of the Church was not contaminated by heresy.* From the earliest time of which we have record the Church sought to prevent heresy being taught and the faithful from believing it. Whereas today we tend to see the structural unity of the Church as more important than combatting heresy, in the Early Church it was the other way round. Both the writers of the New Testament and later orthodox Fathers such as Athanasius were prepared to divide the visible Church rather than let heresy prevail.

Thirdly, *it was a church that kept eternity in view.* The early Christians from the New Testament onwards believed that all human beings would be resurrected to a new form of bodily existence at the end of time, but the almost universal consensus was that there would be an eternal divide between those who would enjoy this new form of existence with God forever in heaven, and those who would suffer eternal punishment forever in hell.

Fourthly, *it was a church that was religiously exclusive*. The early Christians believed, as their Jewish forebears had done, that there was only one true God, who for them was the Triune God who had become incarnate in Christ, and that to worship any other god was idolatry. This meant as Larry Hurtado puts it, that Christianity was the 'destroyer of the gods.'[38] In the words of Lee Gatiss:

> Every convert to Christianity was a loss to the pagan world. The old gods were destroyed as Christianity advanced, which was not true when people simply switched allegiance from one pagan god or goddess to another, in a pluralistic culture that was happy with huge diversity.[39]

Fifthly, *it was an evangelistic church*. Because it was religiously exclusive and believed that the only way to guarantee an eternity spent in heaven rather than hell was through faith in Christ, the early Christians sought to convert everyone they could (which was not something pagan religions sought to do). Furthermore,

---

[38] Larry Hurtado, *Destroyer of the Gods – Early Christian Distinctiveness in the Roman World* (Waco: Baylor University Press, 2016).

[39] Lee Gatiss (ed), *Gospel Flourishing in a Time of Confusion* (Watford: Church Society, 2019), p. 71.

it was the ordinary Christians who did most of the evangelizing. In the words of Kenneth Latourette:

> ... the chief agent in the expansion of Christianity appears not to have been those who made it a profession or made it a major part of their occupation, but men and women who carried on their livelihood in some purely secular manner and spoke of their faith to those they met in a natural fashion.[40]

In addition, as well as being an evangelistic church it was also an apologetic church in the sense that it was a church that took seriously the need to engage in apologetics aimed at showing (a) why Christians were not the 'bad guys' and (b) why Christianity was the true religion while paganism and Judaism were not.

Sixthly, *it was a church that cared for those in need*, both inside and outside the Christian community. They gave alms to the poor and cared for the sick and when the plague came and those who could fled the Christians stayed and cared for the sick and dying, even at the cost of their own lives. In the words of Paul Johnson, they created 'a miniature welfare state in a society which for the most part lacked social services.'[41]

This kind of loving action gave credibility to Christian teaching and made such an impact that the apostate

---

[40] Kenneth Latourette, *A History of the Expansion of Christianity, vol.1* (New York: Harper & Brothers, 1937), p. 116.

[41] Paul Johnson, *A History of Christianity* (New York: Athanaeum, 1976), p. 75.

Emperor Julian exhorted pagan priests to follow their example because it was the 'moral character, even if pretended' of the Christian that led people to desert the pagan gods.

Seventhly, *it was a church that welcomed everybody, but made very high demands on believers.* The early Christians welcomed people from both sexes, all nations and all social classes (see Galatians 3:28), but unlike the members of other religious groups in the Roman Empire 'believing in Christ came with an ethical claim over every second of your day or night and a set of orthodox doctrinal beliefs.'[42] Furthermore, if a Christian departed from orthodox belief or right ethical behaviour (which included an absolute restriction of sexual intercourse to heterosexual marriage) they would, as we have seen, be disciplined and only restored to full communion if they repented of their wrongdoing.

In addition, although it was not the case that all (or most) early Christians faced persecution or were martyred, it was expected that being a Christian meant standing firm in the face of persecution when it did come and, if necessary, choosing death rather than apostasy.

What is also worth noting is that not only was this the kind of church that triumphed in the face of the challenges of the early centuries, but it also this kind of church that has been successful in spreading the

---

[42] Gatiss, p.72.

Christian faith successfully in every generation since, and it is still this kind of church that is growing today in places such as Southeast Asia, Sub-Saharan Africa and South America.

In terms of the Church of England, it is worth noting that the last time the Church of England saw significant growth was in the immediate post war period, and this was a period which was marked by a renewed commitment within the Church both to traditional Christian orthodoxy, and to evangelism in the wake of the 1945 report *Towards the Conversion of England*.[43] By contrast, it was when the Church of England began to lose its grip on orthodox theology and ethics in the 1960s, and began to emphasise social and political action at the expense of evangelism, that the Church of England began to enter into its present period of decline.[44]

The message seems clear. We know the kind of church God wills to use to fulfil the great commission. Given that is the case, the message to the bishops of the Church of England seems equally clear. If they want the Church of England to endure and triumph in the face of the contemporary challenges we have just looked at, then then they need to do what they can to see that the Church of England is this kind of church.

---

[43] The Archbishops' Commission on Evangelism, *Towards the Conversion of England* (London: The Press and Publications Board of the Church Assembly, 1945).
[44] See Adrian Hastings, *A History of Christianity in England 1920-1985* (London: Fount 1987), parts V and VI.

The agenda for bishops today and in the future

The question that then arises is what can bishops do to see that the Church of England is this kind of church?

The first answer to this question is that the proposals that have been leaked to the press for a reordering of the episcopate involving 'non territorial missionary bishops' and 'non diocesan episcopal roles to speak into particular issues' and giving suffragan bishops a 'territorial focus'[45] are ecclesiologically problematic, unnecessary and irrelevant.

They are ecclesiologically problematic because, as we have seen, from New Testament times onwards the God given role of bishops has been to exercise the oversight of the clergy and laity in a particular geographical area. For example, James was made Bishop of Jerusalem (not Bishop for Jewish believers) and Titus was made Bishop of Crete (not Bishop for the Pauline mission).

Obviously, bishops retain their orders and are still therefore bishops if they retire from this role and move on to do something else. Thus, Michael Marshall was still a bishop when he headed up the national Springboard initiative with Michael Green and Tom Wright was still a bishop when he returned to academia. A bishop without a specific territorial responsibility is therefore not an impossibility.

---

[45] See Madeleine Davies, 'Radical Reform Ahead if Top-Level Plan Adopted', *Church Times*, 11 February 2002, pp. 2-3.

However, what it is not right to do is to deliberately create a form of episcopacy that has no responsibility for shepherding the flock in a particular area. Some Orthodox churches have done this, but they have not been right to do so because doing this means giving someone the title 'bishop' without giving them the episcopal responsibility that properly goes with it. Furthermore, this idea also clearly goes against Canons C17, 18 and 20 which, as we have seen describe the role of bishops in specifically diocesan terms.

They are unnecessary as far as suffragan bishops are concerned because all suffragan bishops already have a 'territorial focus' in that they are the suffragan bishops of a particular diocese. The PEVs are often seen as an exception to this rule, but in fact, as we have seen, they are suffragans of the dioceses of Canterbury, York and London who operate in other dioceses with permission as suffragans of the diocesan bishops in those dioceses. If what the leaked paper really means is that all suffragans should be area bishops, this would be problematic for dioceses such as Rochester or Bristol where an area scheme would not be appropriate.

They are irrelevant because there is no evidence that the present arrangements for bishops in the Church of England prevent them from acting as 'good-enough' bishops and there is equally no evidence that playing around with episcopacy in the way proposed is necessary to enable bishops to help the Church of England to become the kind of church God wills to use to fulfil the Great Commission in today's world.

The second answer is that there is clear action that bishops can take individually and collectively as those with episcopal jurisdiction to help the Church of England become this kind of church.

First, in the face of the idolatry of modern Western secular thought, the beliefs held by members of non-Christian religions and the heresy of unconditional divine acceptance and affirmation has come to infect much of the Western Church, the bishops need to teach clearly and with conviction the truth about who God is and what he has done, the truth summarised in the Catechism in the *Book of Common Prayer* and expounded by Luther in his *Small Catechism* of 1529.

In the former we read:

> Catechist. Rehearse the Articles of thy Belief.
>
> Answer. I believe in God the Father Almighty, Maker of heaven and earth:
>
> And in Jesus Christ his only Son our Lord, Who was conceived by the Holy Ghost, Born of the Virgin Mary, Suffered under Pontius Pilate, Was crucified, dead, and buried: He descended into hell; The third day he rose again from the dead; He ascended into heaven, And sitteth at the right hand of God the Father Almighty; From thence he shall come to judge the quick and the dead.
>
> I believe in the Holy Ghost; The holy Catholick Church; The Communion of Saints; The

Forgiveness of sins; The Resurrection of the body, And the life everlasting. Amen.

Question. What dost thou chiefly learn in these Articles of thy Belief?

Answer. First, I learn to believe in God the Father, who hath made me, and all the world.

Secondly, in God the Son, who hath redeemed me, and all mankind.

Thirdly, in God the Holy Ghost, who sanctifieth me, and all the elect people of God.

In the latter we read:

The First Article

I believe in God the Father Almighty, Maker of heaven and earth.

What does this mean?

I believe that God has made me and all creatures; that He has given me my body and soul, eyes, ears and all my members, my reason and all my senses, and still preserves them; that He richly and daily provides me with food and clothing, home and family, property and goods, and all that I need to support this body and life; that He protects me from all danger, guards and keeps me from all evil; and all this purely out of fatherly, divine goodness and mercy, without any merit or worthiness in me; for all which I am in duty bound to thank and praise, to serve and obey Him. This is most certainly true.

The Second Article

I believe in Jesus Christ, His only Son our Lord; Who was conceived by the Holy Spirit, born of the virgin Mary, suffered under Pontius Pilate, was crucified, died and was buried. He descended into hell; the third day He rose again from the dead; He ascended into heaven and is seated at the right hand of God the Father almighty; from there He shall come to judge the living and the dead.

What does this mean?

I believe that Jesus Christ is true God, begotten of the Father from eternity, and also true man, born of the virgin Mary; and that He is my Lord, Who has redeemed me, a lost and condemned creature, purchased and won me from all sins, from death and from the power of the devil; not with gold or silver, but with His holy, precious blood, and with His innocent suffering and death; in order that I might be His own, live under Him in His kingdom, and serve Him in everlasting righteousness, innocence and blessedness; even as He is risen from the dead, lives and reigns to all eternity. This is most certainly true.

The Third Article

I believe in the Holy Spirit, the holy Christian Church, the communion of saints, the forgiveness of sins, the resurrection of the body, and the life everlasting. Amen.

What does this mean?

I believe that I cannot by my own reason or strength believe in Jesus Christ, my Lord, or come to Him; but the Holy Ghost has called me by the Gospel, enlightened me with His gifts, sanctified and kept me in the true faith; just as He calls, gathers, enlightens and sanctifies the whole Christian Church on earth and keeps it with Jesus Christ in the one true faith. In this Christian Church He daily and richly forgives me and all believers all our sins; and at the last day He will raise up me and all the dead, and will grant me and all believers in Christ eternal life. This is most certainly true.[46]

Those in the Church of England need to know and hold to these basic Christian truths and share them with others, and so the bishops, as those called to be the primary teachers of the Church, need to be constantly teaching them. It is important that bishops comment on the issues of the day both inside and outside the Church, but the most important thing they are called to

---

[46] Martin Luther, *The Small Catechism,* text at The Evangelical Lutheran Synod, https://els.org/beliefs/luthers-small-catechism/part-2-the-apostles-creed/.

do is to instruct the faithful in the fundamental truths concerning God's identity and his mighty acts of creation, redemption and sanctification. History shows that when the faithful are confident about these truths then the Church will flourish.

Secondly, in view of the fact that many people both in the world and in the Church are focused on the life of this present world, and those who do believe in life after death increasingly assume that it will involve the same outcome for everyone, bishops need to teach clearly and with conviction the meaning of Christian belief in 'the life everlasting.' In the words of the seventeenth century bishop John Pearson, they need to declare:

> I do fully and freely assent unto this as a most necessary and infallible truth, that the unjust after their resurrection and condemnation shall be tormented for their sins in hell, and shall so be continued in torments for ever, so as neither the justice of God shall ever cease to inflict them, nor the persons of the wicked cease to subsist and suffer them; and that the just after their resurrection and absolution shall as the blessed of the Father obtain the inheritance, and as the servants of God enter into their masters joy, freed from all possibility of death sin and sorrow, filled with all conceivable and inconceivable fulness of happiness, confirmed in an absolute security of an eternal enjoyment

and so shall they continue with God and with
the Lamb for ever more.[47]

In today's world Christians are often shy about
mentioning hell, believing that they will be seen as
cruel and heartless if they teach about its reality.
However, if hell is real, then what is in fact cruel and
heartless is not to warn people about its existence so
that they may do what is necessary to avoid it.

Likewise, as Lewis comments:

> We are very shy nowadays of even mentioning
> heaven. We are afraid of the jeer about 'pie in
> the sky,' and of being told that we are trying to
> 'escape' from the duty of making a happy world
> here and now into dreams of a happy world
> elsewhere. But either there is 'pie in the sky' or
> there is not. If there is not, then Christianity is
> false, for this doctrine is woven into its whole
> fabric. If there is, then this truth, like any other,
> must be faced, whether it is useful at political
> meetings or no. Again, we are afraid that
> heaven is a bribe and that if we make it our goal
> we shall no longer be disinterested. It is not so.
> Heaven offers nothing that a mercenary soul
> can desire. It is safe to tell the pure in heart that
> they shall see God, for only the pure in heart
> want to. There are rewards that do not sully
> motives. A man's love for a woman is not
> mercenary because he wants to marry her, nor

---

[47] John Pearson, *An Exposition of the Creed* (London:
George Bell, 1902), p. 600-601.

his love for poetry mercenary because he wants to read it, nor his love of exercise less disinterested because he wants to run and leap and walk. Love, by definition, seeks to enjoy its object.[48]

People both inside and outside the Church need to know the truth that 'here we have no lasting city, but we seek the city which is to come' (Hebrews 13:14) so that they me live rightly in the light of it and so the bishops need to be clearly and constantly teaching it to them.

Thirdly, the bishops need to teach clearly and with conviction that the only guaranteed way to enjoy a blessed eternity is through faith in Jesus Christ. This is because, as Article XVIII puts it:

> They also are to be had accursed that presume to say that every man shall be saved by the law or sect which he professeth, so that he be diligent to frame his life according to that law and the light of nature. For Holy Scripture doth set out to us only the name of Jesus Christ, whereby men must be saved.

In the words of Bishop Harold Browne in his commentary on this article, what it warns against is that:

> .... latitudinarianism, which makes all creeds and all communions alike, saying that all men

---

[48] C S Lewis, *The Problem of Pain* (Glasgow: Fount, 1978), pp. 132-133.

may be saved by their own sect, so they shape their lives according to it, and according to the law of nature. The ground, on which it protests against this view of matters, is that the Scriptures set forth no other name but Christ's whereby we may be saved. The opinion here condemned therefore, is not a charitable hope, that persons, who have never heard of Christ, or who have been bred in ignorance or error, may not be inevitably excluded from the benefit of His atonement; but that cold indifference to faith and truth, which would rest satisfied and leave them in their errors, instead of striving to bring them to faith in Christ and to His Body the Church, to which alone the promises of the Gospel are made, and to which, by actual revelation God's mercies are annexed.[49]

Because the sort of latitudinarianism to which Browne refers is common in both the world and the Church today, bishops need to bear clear witness to the biblical exclusivism of historic Christianity declaring clearly and with conviction '....there is salvation in no one else, for there is no other name under heaven given among men by which we must be saved' (Acts 4:12).

Fourthly, because the only guarantee of salvation is through faith in Christ, bishops must be striving to bring people to faith in him. As leaders of mission, they

---

[49] Harold Browne, *An Exposition of the Thirty Nine Articles* (London: John W Parker, 1847), p. 440.

must be evangelists themselves and must also teach and equip the clergy and laity to be evangelists as well.

In their teaching they must explain clearly both the nature and aim of evangelism.

In the words of *Towards the Conversion of England*, they must explain that:

> To evangelise is so to present Christ Jesus in the power of the Holy Spirit, that men shall come to put their trust in God through Him, to accept him as their Saviour, and to serve Him as their King in the fellowship of His Church. [50]

They must also explain, (a) that the aim of evangelism:

> .... is Conversion. Conversion is the reorientation of life from self to God through Christ Jesus. Conversion may be sudden: a revolutionary experience, like a revealing flash of lightning, which enables the convert to commemorate a spiritual birthday. Or conversion may be gradual: an evolutionary development like the dawn of day, or the miracle of the harvest field [Mark 4:26-29]. But whether sudden or gradual, it is the birth right of every child of God to be converted, or (in St. Pauls' phrase) to 'be *alive* unto God in Christ Jesus our Lord' [Romans 6:11]. Short of this

---

[50] *Towards the Conversion of England*, p. 1.

there is no stopping place for the evangelist, no sure resting place for the convert.[51]

(b) that conversion generally involves 'two stages which, though logically successive, are generally intertwined in practice.' [52]

> The first or preliminary stage consists in arousing the interest of those to whom the message is being delivered - meeting their objections and showing how the gospel finds men just where they are, satisfying their deepest needs.

> The other stage is the actual bringing the convert to the point of decision - that personal abandonment to the divine will in purpose which is involved with the acceptance of Christ Jesus saviour and king. This is primarily a matter of the individual will. While, therefore, all evangelism is in essence a personal ministry, this is more markedly so in the second stage of evangelism. For the affecting of a conversion under the operation of the Holy Spirit, the direct and immediate contact of a person with a person almost always seems to be called for.[53]

Fifthly, bishops must teach and practice care for those in need both inside and outside the Church. Such care

---

[51] *Towards the Conversion of England*, p. 36.
[52] *Towards the Conversion of England*, p. 37.
[53] *Towards the Conversion of England*, p. 38.

is required as obedience to the command to 'love your neighbour as yourself (Leviticus 19:18, Luke 10:25-27), but also as a necessary accompaniment to evangelism.

This is because, while the verbal proclamation and defence of the intellectual truth of the Christian faith are a necessary part of evangelism, they are not necessarily the best place to start. In the post-modern consumer society we now inhabit, claims to be declaring the truth about the human condition are regarded with widespread suspicion in the same way that we regard with suspicion the claims made by advertisers and other people who are trying to 'sell' us things.

As Graham Tomlin argues in his book *The Provocative Church*,[54] what this means is that people will only take Christian truth claims seriously and therefore be open to start on the path to conversion if these truth claims can be seen to be embodied in a plausible fashion in the life of the Christian community. To put it another way, non-Christians will only take the Christian message seriously if Christians don't just 'talk the talk' but also 'walk the walk.'

In addition, Christians who 'walk the walk' are the best antidote to the claim that Christians are the 'bad guys.' People will find implausible to believe that Christians are truly the bad guys if their practical care for those in need shows otherwise.

---

[54] Graham Tomlin, *The Provocative Church* (London: SPCK, 2002).

However, bishops must explain that walking the walk is not a substitute for 'talking the talk.' Christians still need to explain to non-Christians that they are caring for others not because they are naturally nice people but because they have met the one true God in Jesus Christ and have found the fulness of life he promised (John 10:10) in living in obedience to his commands. Tomlin's argument is that Christian care for those in need will provoke people to ask questions (hence the title of his book) and that will give the opportunity to talk to people about the nature and truth of the Christian message.

Sixthly, bishops must teach that while all types of people are to be welcomed into the Church, this does not mean that all types of behaviour are to be accepted within the Church. This is something that the Church has never believed from New Testament times onwards. On the contrary, it has always been held that there is a God given pattern of right behaviour to which Christians must adhere. Christians are called to be God-determined rather than self-determined people and that means living in a particular way. We can see this for example in the exhortations contained in Paul's letters. Thus, Paul tells the Ephesian Christians in Ephesians 5:1-20:

> Therefore be imitators of God, as beloved children. And walk in love, as Christ loved us and gave himself up for us, a fragrant offering and sacrifice to God.

But fornication and all impurity or covetousness must not even be named among you, as is fitting among saints. Let there be no filthiness, nor silly talk, nor levity, which are not fitting; but instead let there be thanksgiving. Be sure of this, that no fornicator or impure man, or one who is covetous (that is, an idolater), has any inheritance in the kingdom of Christ and of God. Let no one deceive you with empty words, for it is because of these things that the wrath of God comes upon the sons of disobedience. Therefore do not associate with them, for once you were darkness, but now you are light in the Lord; walk as children of light (for the fruit of light is found in all that is good and right and true), and try to learn what is pleasing to the Lord. Take no part in the unfruitful works of darkness, but instead expose them. For it is a shame even to speak of the things that they do in secret; but when anything is exposed by the light it becomes visible, for anything that becomes visible is light. Therefore it is said,

'Awake, O sleeper, and arise from the dead,
and Christ shall give you light.'

Look carefully then how you walk, not as unwise men but as wise, making the most of the time, because the days are evil. Therefore do not be foolish, but understand what the will of the Lord is. And do not get drunk with wine, for that is debauchery; but be filled with the Spirit, addressing one another in psalms and hymns and spiritual songs, singing and making melody to the Lord with all your heart, always and for everything giving thanks in the name of our Lord Jesus Christ to God the Father.

As Paul's words make clear, adhering to the Christian ethic in obedience to God involves doing (or not doing) many different things, but as we have seen during this study, part of what it involves is living as the man or woman God created us to be rather than choosing our own sexual identity and only engaging in sexual intercourse within its God-given setting of heterosexual marriage.

This in turn means that bishops need to teach, over and against the prevailing ethos of Western society, and even at the price of being labelled transphobes and homophobes, that gender transition and same-sex relationships are not acceptable forms of Christian behaviour. Transgender people and those in same-sex relationships must be unconditionally welcomed into the Church just like anyone else, but the Christian community needs to encourage them, as part of submission to the kingship of Christ, to live according to their biological sex and abstain from same-sex sexual activity.

Seventhly, bishops need to take seriously their calling to 'banish and drive away all erroneous and strange doctrine contrary to God's word; and both privately and openly to call upon and encourage others to do the same' and also to 'correct and punish' those who are 'unquiet, disobedient and criminous.' For the sake of the spiritual health of the flock and the integrity of its witness to the watching world, bishops need to refute heretical ideas, and use their powers of jurisdiction to discipline both those who teach heresy and those who encourage or practice ungodly forms of behaviour. As we have seen in the course of this study this is what bishops have been called to do since apostolic times and what they still need to do today.

Finally, bishops, as the senior presbyters within the Church, need to select, train, and appoint other presbyters, deacons, and lay ministers of various kinds to work with them to carry out the tasks just outlined. As we have seen, this is what Timothy and Titus were instructed to do, and it is what bishops still need to do today. A bishop, however godly and however talented, cannot transform a diocese on their own, but they can do it if they have godly ministers working with them.

What bishops need to do after *Living in Love and Faith*

In the very near future the bishops of the Church of England will have to decide what action to take following the *Living in Love and Faith* process.

The basic answer is clear, what the bishops ought to do is to affirm orthodox Christian teaching on sexual identity and practice by commending to the Church of England something along the lines of the *Nashville Statement on Human Sexuality* set out below:

Preamble

> Evangelical Christians at the dawn of the twenty-first century find themselves living in a period of historic transition. As Western culture has become increasingly post-Christian, it has embarked upon a massive revision of what it means to be a human being. By and large the spirit of our age no longer discerns or delights in the beauty of God's design for human life. Many deny that God created human beings for his glory, and that his good purposes for us include our personal and physical design as male and female. It is common to think that human identity as male and female is not part of God's beautiful plan, but is, rather, an expression of an individual's autonomous preferences. The pathway to full and lasting joy through God's good design for his creatures is thus replaced by the path of shortsighted alternatives that, sooner or later, ruin human life and dishonor God.

> This secular spirit of our age presents a great challenge to the Christian church. Will the church of the Lord Jesus Christ lose her biblical conviction, clarity, and courage, and blend into the spirit of the age? Or will she hold fast to the

word of life, draw courage from Jesus, and unashamedly proclaim his way as the way of life? Will she maintain her clear, counter-cultural witness to a world that seems bent on ruin?

We are persuaded that faithfulness in our generation means declaring once again the true story of the world and of our place in it—particularly as male and female. Christian Scripture teaches that there is but one God who alone is Creator and Lord of all. To him alone, every person owes gladhearted thanksgiving, heart-felt praise, and total allegiance. This is the path not only of glorifying God, but of knowing ourselves. To forget our Creator is to forget who we are, for he made us for himself. And we cannot know ourselves truly without truly knowing him who made us. We did not make ourselves. We are not our own. Our true identity, as male and female persons, is given by God. It is not only foolish, but hopeless, to try to make ourselves what God did not create us to be.

We believe that God's design for his creation and his way of salvation serve to bring him the greatest glory and bring us the greatest good. God's good plan provides us with the greatest freedom. Jesus said he came that we might have life and have it in overflowing measure. He is for us and not against us. Therefore, in the hope of serving Christ's church and witnessing publicly to the good purposes of God for human sexuality revealed in Christian Scripture, we offer the following affirmations and denials.

Article 1

WE AFFIRM that God has designed marriage to be a covenantal, sexual, procreative, lifelong union of one man and one woman, as husband and wife, and is meant to signify the covenant love between Christ and his bride the church.

WE DENY that God has designed marriage to be a homosexual, polygamous, or polyamorous relationship. We also deny that marriage is a mere human contract rather than a covenant made before God.

Article 2
WE AFFIRM that God's revealed will for all people is chastity outside of marriage and fidelity within marriage.

WE DENY that any affections, desires, or commitments ever justify sexual intercourse before or outside marriage; nor do they justify any form of sexual immorality.

Article 3
WE AFFIRM that God created Adam and Eve, the first human beings, in his own image, equal before God as persons, and distinct as male and female.

WE DENY that the divinely ordained differences between male and female render them unequal in dignity or worth.

Article 4
WE AFFIRM that divinely ordained differences between male and female reflect God's original creation design and are meant for human good and human flourishing.

WE DENY that such differences are a result of the Fall or are a tragedy to be overcome.

Article 5
WE AFFIRM that the differences between male and female reproductive structures are integral to God's design for self-conception as male or female.

WE DENY that physical anomalies or psychological conditions nullify the God-appointed link between biological sex and self-conception as male or female.

Article 6

WE AFFIRM that those born with a physical disorder of sex development are created in the image of God and have dignity and worth equal to all other image-bearers. They are acknowledged by our Lord Jesus in his words about 'eunuchs who were born that way from their mother's womb.' With all others they are welcome as faithful followers of Jesus Christ and should embrace their biological sex insofar as it may be known.

WE DENY that ambiguities related to a person's biological sex render one incapable of living a fruitful life in joyful obedience to Christ.

Article 7

WE AFFIRM that self-conception as male or female should be defined by God's holy purposes in creation and redemption as revealed in Scripture.

WE DENY that adopting a homosexual or transgender self-conception is consistent with God's holy purposes in creation and redemption.

Article 8

WE AFFIRM that people who experience sexual attraction for the same sex may live a rich and fruitful life pleasing to God through faith in Jesus Christ, as they, like all Christians, walk in purity of life.

WE DENY that sexual attraction for the same sex is part of the natural goodness of God's original creation, or that it puts a person outside the hope of the gospel.

Article 9
WE AFFIRM that sin distorts sexual desires by directing them away from the marriage covenant and toward sexual immorality— a distortion that includes both heterosexual and homosexual immorality.

WE DENY that an enduring pattern of desire for sexual immorality justifies sexually immoral behavior.

Article 10
WE AFFIRM that it is sinful to approve of homosexual immorality or transgenderism and that such approval constitutes an essential departure from Christian faithfulness and witness.

WE DENY that the approval of homosexual immorality or transgenderism is a matter of moral indifference about which otherwise faithful Christians should agree to disagree.

Article 11
WE AFFIRM our duty to speak the truth in love at all times, including when we speak to or about one another as male or female.
WE DENY any obligation to speak in such ways that dishonor God's design of his image bearers as male and female.

Article 12
WE AFFIRM that the grace of God in Christ gives both merciful pardon and transforming power, and that this pardon and power enable a follower of Jesus to put to death sinful desires and to walk in a manner worthy of the Lord.

WE DENY that the grace of God in Christ is insufficient to forgive all sexual sins and to give power for holiness to every believer who feels drawn into sexual sin.

Article 13
WE AFFIRM that the grace of God in Christ enables sinners to forsake transgender self-conception and by divine forbearance to accept the God-ordained link between one's biological sex and one's self-conception as male or female.

WE DENY that the grace of God in Christ sanctions self-conceptions that are at odds with God's revealed will.

Article 14
WE AFFIRM that Christ Jesus has come into the world to save sinners and that through Christ's death and resurrection forgiveness of sins and eternal life are available to every person who repents of sin and trusts in Christ alone as Savior, Lord, and supreme treasure.

WE DENY that the Lord's arm is too short to save or that any sinner is beyond his reach.[55]

In addition, the bishops also ought to propose a revision of the Church of England's current discipline so that services to mark gender transition are no longer permitted, so that those who have undergone gender transition are not permitted to be ordained, and so that lay ministers as well as ordained ministers are expected to abstain from both gender-transition and same-sex relationships.

Moving in this direction would bring about howls of protest from both inside and outside the Church of England, but the bishops should ignore this and act in this way anyway, simply because it is the right thing to do.

It is, however, sadly possible that the majority of the bishops, with the support of the General Synod, will eventually seek to move the Church of England in the

---

[55] *The Nashville Statement* at https://cbmw.org/nashville-statement/.

same sort of liberal direction already taken by The Episcopal Church, the Anglican Church in Canada, the Scottish Episcopal Church and the Church in Wales.

If this happens what should orthodox bishops do? The answer depends on exactly what is proposed.

If what is proposed is the establishment of a 'pastoral accommodation' allowing clergy to bless same-sex relationships and civil same-sex marriages on a permissive basis, then orthodox bishops will need to work to establish the right for bishops to not allow such blessings in their dioceses and for a system of delegated episcopal oversight to be created which would allow clergy and parishes who did not want to allow such blessings to come under the jurisdiction of a bishop who took the same position (with reciprocal arrangements for liberal parishes whose bishop did not give permission for such blessings to take place).

If what is proposed is a change to Canon B.30 which would change the Church of England's definition of marriage and allow same-sex marriages to take place, then orthodox bishops will need to work to establish a third province for orthodox Anglicans within the Church of England, alongside the existing provinces of Canterbury and York. This province, which parishes would be able to opt into by means of a vote by their Parochial Church Councils, would have its own bishops, its own convocation, and its own code of Canon law, and as a result it would be able to give robust long-term protection to clergy and parishes who wish to adhere to traditional Church of England teaching and practice and provide a base from which the re-evangelization of the rest of the Church of England and the English nation might take place in God's good time. [56]

If they are not able to bring either of the two previous options to pass, then orthodox bishops like other orthodox clergy and laity, should be prepared to consider leaving the Church of England and forming a new orthodox Anglican province outside the Church of England along the lines of ACNA in North America, which would provide a home for orthodox Anglicans in England, Wales and Scotland.[57]

The formation of this new province would mean establishing parallel episcopal jurisdictions in these three countries. As we saw in chapter 12, such parallel jurisdictions should ideally not exist, but they are legitimate when a church and/or bishop in a particular place departs from Christian orthodoxy in matters of belief or conduct to such a serious extent that faithful Christians have no alternative but to separate themselves from that church or that bishop. In this situation it will be necessary to create a new church

---

[56] For a detailed study of these two options see Martin Davie and Stephen Hofmeyr, *Visibly Different* (London: CEEC 2002), Chs. 6-7.

[57] Hopefully, the Free Church of England and the Anglican Mission in England would agree to become part of this new province.

with its own bishops and hence to create a new parallel episcopal jurisdiction.

This is exactly the situation which the proposed new province in England, Wales and Scotland would be designed to meet. The Church in Wales and the Scottish Episcopal Church and their bishops have already accepted same-sex marriages and in the situation envisaged the Church of England and the majority of its bishops would have done the same. Creating a parallel jurisdiction would thus be the right thing to do.

Bishops in this new province would have legitimate episcopal jurisdictions in the Church in England, and would thus be the heirs of James, Ignatius, Athanasius, Augustine, and Cranmer, even if they no longer possessed episcopal jurisdiction in the Church of England.

What we have to pray for, of course, is that none of the options just described will prove necessary, but that the bishops as a whole will act as the shepherds they are called to be by protecting those in the Church of England from the influence of the modern Western ideology of self-determination and the ungodly views of sexual identity and sexual behaviour that flow from it.

To this end we should pray constantly for all the bishops of the Church of England, using the prayer for a new bishop in the 1662 *Ordinal.*

> Almighty God and most merciful Father, who of thine infinite goodness hast given thine only

and dearly beloved Son Jesus Christ, to be our Redeemer and the Author of everlasting life; who, after that he had made perfect our redemption by his death, and was ascended into heaven, poured down his gifts abundantly upon men, making some Apostles, some Prophets, some Evangelists, some Pastors and Doctors, to the edifying and making perfect his Church: Grant, we beseech thee, to these thy servants such grace, that they may evermore be ready to spread abroad thy Gospel, the glad tidings of reconciliation with thee; and use the authority given them, not to destruction, but to salvation; not to hurt, but to help: so that as wise and faithful servants, giving to thy family their portion in due season, they may at last be received into everlasting joy; through Jesus Christ our Lord, who with thee and the Holy Ghost liveth and reigneth, one God, world without end. Amen

Other Latimer Publications

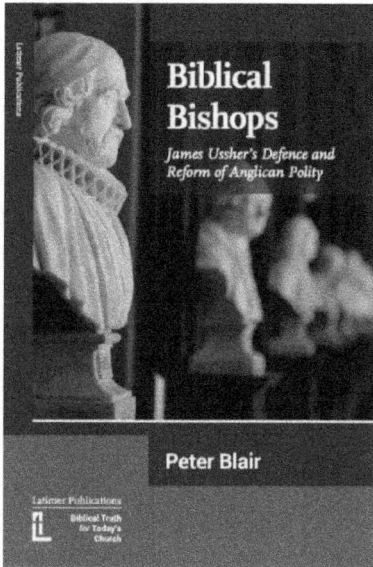

As fissures emerge within the worldwide Anglican communion, the principle and praxis of episcopacy have never been more pertinent. For some Anglicans, bishops are essential for the church. For others, they are something of a necessary evil; baggage from the English reformation that we might be better off without.

These concerns are nothing new. In the seventeenth century, debates surrounding the validity and authority of bishops abounded. Into those debates wrote James Ussher, archbishop of Armagh and Primate of All Ireland. Ussher was a remarkable figure: a preeminent historian, biblical scholar, and theologian, respected by English puritans and Irish Jesuits alike. As is often the case with such luminaries, various camps have claimed

Ussher as their own; whether they be puritan, high church, or anglo-catholic.

By studying Ussher's ecclesiastical career and his two works on church government, this study assesses Ussher's episcopalian convictions, particularly regarding the validity and authority of bishops. In doing so, it hopes to reintroduce Ussher to the evangelical Anglican world, and demonstrate that episcopacy is not a necessary evil, but a force for good in the church of God.

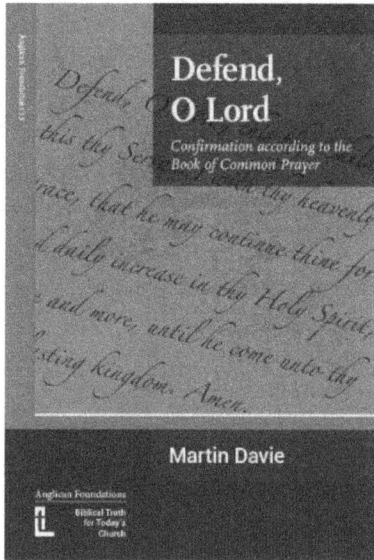

Defend, O Lord

Confirmation according to the Book of Common Prayer

Martin Davie

A key way in which the benefits of the work of Christ are conveyed to those who respond to the gospel with repentance and faith is through the two rites of 'Christian initiation': baptism and confirmation. In baptism we die to our old life of sin and death and rise to a new life with God which will be fully revealed at the resurrection of the dead at the end of time.

In confirmation we reaffirm the promises which were made at our baptism, and we are given strength through the Spirit to live the new life we have been given in baptism, and protection from all that would turn us away from God.

The Church of England's normative confirmation service, to which the *Common Worship* services are authorised alternatives, is the confirmation service in the 1662 *Book of Common Prayer*.

This little book provides an introduction to the 1662 service. It describes how confirmation developed in the Early Church and during the Middle Ages and how the Prayer Book confirmation service developed after the Reformation. It also provides a detailed commentary on the Prayer Book service, and answers the ten key questions people today generally ask about confirmation.

IN THE ST ANTHOLIN LECTURE SERIES

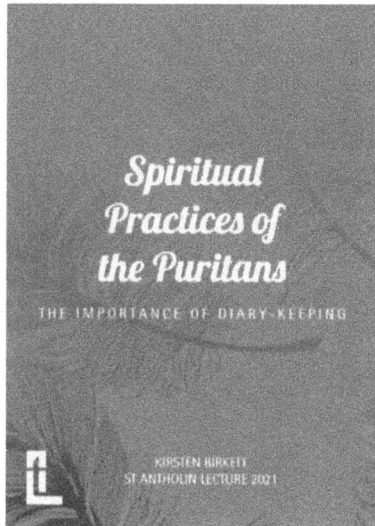

The Puritans wished to live godly lives in heart and thought as well as action. One of the tools they utilised in training their hearts and minds was the practice of diary-writing. In this short overview we see the theory of Puritan diary-writing as worked out by John Beadle, and the inspiring example of the sixteenth-century Puritan Richard Rogers writing about his life.

www.ingramcontent.com/pod-product-compliance
Lightning Source LLC
Chambersburg PA
CBHW020955030426
42339CB00005B/107